UMBRAGEOUS EMBERS

To order additional copies of this title visit www.toddfabozzi.com.

Book Design by Melissa Mykal Batalin.
Back cover photo by Nicholas Lue.

The Troy Book Makers in Troy, NY.
www.thetroybookmakers.com

ISBN: 978-1-933994-54-3

UMBRAGEOUS EMBERS

TODD FABOZZI

To America,
which is the primary subject of this book,
and to my children,
Marino and Giana, with all my love.

Contents

"It's not dark yet...but it's getting there."
– Bob Dylan

UMBRAGEOUS EMBERS

bio

before I introduce our esteemed guest
let me tell you a bit about him

he's a:
drummer, writer
laugher, lover
father, fighter
preacher, teacher
talker, walker
planner, geographer
photographer, cartographer
people watcher, gossip fodder
entertainer, illuminator
weight lifter, shape shifter
vision seeker, nose tweaker
innovator, apostate traitor
trip taker, muckraker
malcontent, misanthrope
thinks he knows it, thinker poet...

and he's been quite busy lately
picking pecks of pickled peppers.

poetry reading

poets of the world
gather to sing their songs

they bring notebooks
and tell tales of pain and joy
sorrow they can't shake
a trauma
a loved one
unleashing the barbed burrs
burrowed in their guts

there are revolutionaries
with their notes of insurgent dissent
practicing the art of opposition
poking poems at the status quo

they know the cities, the desolation
and see the sprawl for what it is
the gates and isolation
that say keep out
and know your station

they feel the fog of propaganda
and hear lies for what they are

they know war
is a shell game with people
and the ones in power
aren't the ones getting killed

they know about personal freedom
and how the amendments are fading away

and they know about hypocrisy
and doing time for getting high

and they can feel the force of nature
and they respect it like it's God

so they gather, all the poets
to bare their souls
and share their rhymes

they are the insane voice of sanity
in sorrowful insane voiceless times.

the critic

a famous literary critic
is giving a talk at the Writers Institute

he has a reputation:
they say he swings an unmerciful axe
at the tallest trees

he's hacked and chopped
DeLillo, Pynchon, Wolf, and others
hoping to humble
the giant redwoods of American letters

they say he's savage with his opinions
like a crank talk show host
only smarter
and more articulate

he wears his snobbishness
like an English accent
and uses philosophy
and the words of dead white men
to put people in their place

but he's written his own novel now
revealing his true self

like DJs
and some teachers
the critic secretly desires
an other self

and sometimes
at the witching hour
when the candlelight burns low
his venom invective
will hit the page
in inverse proportion
to his secret admirations

but now it's his turn
to leave himself exposed

so he reads his masterpiece
and I listen with attentive care
trying to size up this titan
to verify what makes him so special

but what I hear
are textbook words
perfect in their boredom

and I wait for life to jump from his polished tongue
for him to shake me profoundly, as he might say

yet I wait in vain
and listen
and yawn
as his bleached words of refinement
put me to sleep.

scars

the scars are thick and ridged
veiled
like coded maps of pain
inexplicit

hidden from obvious sight
yet apparent in decoded eyes

ghost pains nonspecific
sometimes in the stomach pit
sometimes between the eyes

the lips try to articulate
but are stuck, hollow
or stutter staccato sobs instead

there is emptiness
and a hopelessness that lingers
in sentimental futility

like carved names on a picnic table
the damaged traces remain

all the disappointing blindness
unaware in its harm
so certain in its ignorance

personal or public
the stones of accreted letdowns
and the boulders of grand malfeasance

layer upon layer
the sedimentary strata
in hidden psychic deposits
the scars of heightened consciousness
forever unhealed behind sensitive eyes.

black gold

it bubbled up from the ground
in a black oily ooze

they stuck their fingers in it
and licked it
and smiled with stained teeth
because it tasted like gold

so they poked big straws in the ground
to suck it out
and bottled it in big barrels
for everyone to drink

it was packed so full of history
eons of condensed rot
that it could spin a dynamo
with supernatural powers

and the supply was endless
or so they thought
a creamy nougat center
spurting to the sky like old faithful
so they built their whole system
to depend on it

and they ignored the dark clouds
on the smog-shroud horizon
accepting pending doom
as a fair price for black magic

and they ignored the subterfuge
in the places it was buried
accepting war
as the necessary price to control it

and with furrowed brows
they dealt with deprivation
as despondent dependants
had their pockets picked
for mobility

and eventually
they were sent back to square one
when the bubbles stopped bubbling
and they were forced to choose
between cornflakes or black gold for breakfast.

witness

I am the eyes at the edge of the room, listening

my tongue can taste truth behind the façade
and smell the scent of insincerity like a hungry wolf

there is constant talking
negotiations to decide futures

the leaded walls contain the tales
with titles unannounced

the politics of the deal
that sets our fate
uninvited to participate

though sometimes
the wind will drop a lucky backstage pass
to a window on the world of our unmaking

and if so, sit and smile
and don't let on
in subversive cover

wear the mask of propriety
that shades your knowing eyes

and listen well
for you have been let in
on secret stories not to hold

but to hand off to the mockingbird
to scatter like winged seeds of a new awareness.

the wild wild west

the congresswoman from Arizona
wants to allow kids to pack heat at school

given all the violent rampages lately—
the mow-downs at a few colleges
a few shopping malls
a few high schools
a few fast-food joints—

she figures
the solution to all this gun violence is
more guns:
get 'em all armed
let 'em shoot it out real good
like in the old days

best way to cut down on violence:
more violence
vigilante justice
won't even need cops anymore
just someone to clean up the bodies
and spread fresh sawdust on the floor
out here in the wild wild west.

just like that

he spends most of his life flying
from one place to another
like a bird without feathers

this is his life, his job
always flying
taking care of business

he's a lonely one
with no friends
and no one to miss him
when he's gone

he's like lots of people
who spend their lives
in the hopeless pursuit
we call making a living
flying from town to town
waiting in airports
waiting in line
getting searched and scanned
in their sox
bored and tired
dreaming of excitement and meaning
wondering in weak moments
if today is the day when
it all goes down in a fiery wreck

sometimes it happens
just like that

one minute you're reading the paper
or dreaming of sunshine
or just minding your own business
and the next moment
you're begging the god you've neglected
to spare your sorry soul

but the lonely flier never had such thoughts
never contemplated loneliness
or mortality
or the cruel hand of fate

he just went about his business
until that fateful day
when his life was cut short in a horrific crash

it happened just like that

and there was only
one mourner at the funeral
only one person in this wide world
who noted his absence
and that was me...
the one who saw him explode
in a blast of green and yellow mucus
here today and gone tomorrow
in a splat across my windshield.

cruising with a shopping cart

the stolen shopping cart contains his world:
a ripped sleeping bag
dirty clothes in plastic bags
and a rusty three-string guitar without a case
surely out of tune

sometimes I see him
propped against the wall
next to his house on wheels
strumming the old thing

it has two holes, instead of one
the second hole, the shape of a boot

he hums away with his far-away stare
singing something old, about Dixie
and beans
and railroads

maybe he was famous once:
maybe there was this glorious fifteen minutes
when his star shone bright

but maybe his luck changed—
it happens to just about everyone

and if you've attained high heights
the fall is farther and harder
always haunted by memory
that time
that height you no longer know

or maybe it was something simpler
and more common place
like a closed factory
and him, too old to move again
too old to go back to school
too old to start over
too old to look for love
or simply too old to care

so he just stands there
every day
wrinkled and weather beaten
life beaten
looking off to some silent somewhere
remembering old stories
and sad songs to
strum away his pain.

#1

they talk about community
but what they mean is exclusion:
their community is patrolled
and surrounded by gates

they talk about sustainability
but what they mean is
how to sustain the status quo
how to keep driving and driving

they talk about freedom
but their world is a prison
with a TV
and a computer
and an electric garage-door

they talk about authentic values
but their world is made of plastic
and images
and propaganda

they look to their leaders
to make them feel like winners
to keep America #1

but their leaders only know
how to take care of their own
and only know one way to get ahead:
it was taught to them at the military academy

it was taught to them in the MBA program
by the world's leading economic philosophers

they were taught it was a virtue to
stand on the backs of others
and look out for #1.

Frankie baby

in the future
there will be people
better than the ordinary others

they will come pre-programmed:
genetically manipulated
to be smarter
stronger
more cunning
and more apt to be
in the upper one percent
that's in control

they will be commercial spin-offs
of super soldiers
and they will have bionic parts
like comic book characters

it will be easy for them
to out maneuver
outrun
outwit
overpower
ordinary humans
in every way...
to crush them like grapes if necessary

but they won't need to

that will be the duty of the drones:
the robot machines
that fly
see
sense
and crawl like mechanical insects
programmed to detect and destroy
on command

and the day may come
when they will do so
let loose
like mad genies out of broken bottles
popping people like pimples
then turning with cold smiles
to teach their creators a lesson
about playing God with fire.

round pegs in square holes

there are those who can't help
but veer toward freedom
seeking to overcome false limits
and superstitious morality
nurtured from the soil of fear

limits on saying what you will
believing what you want
seeking to transcend
by considering off-limit subjects
or stepping outside the bounds

where out of society's fears
grow laws
and victimless victims
and new categories of outlaws
unfit for the norm

filed for seeking freedom
and seeing visions
beyond bland worlds

for stating opposition
and defying conscriptions

for pursuing new sensations
and a derangement of the whitewash

for seeking to circumscribe

bent rules and stale standards
and average ways
of thinking
and saying
and being.

the levee of indifference

it was a category five
pointed right at the Big Easy

a knockout punch of
wind and water
but the worst was still waiting

miscalculations
shortchanged shortcuts
that cut waterfalls
through malfeasant cracks

a torrent into the ninth ward
the poor ward
the better-them-than-us ward

they climbed into attics
with water to their necks

they climbed onto rooftops
and waved frantic arms at no one

they floated like bloated rafts
like garbage in the gutter
the refuse of our inaction
drifting past shrunken wetlands
past oil derricks sucking gold from the earth

they were herded like cattle
the ones with no cars
packed into a football stadium
that on any other given day
was too expensive for them to get in

they prayed and cried
and some died
but there were others who didn't die
though died a different kind of death
wallowing in their excrement

they died of indifference
of racism
of poverty

they died of a broken heart
seeing reality unadorned in America
knowing that
to be black and poor
means you don't matter to them

you are a one-way ticket to wherever

you are a poison trailer

you are lost in the bureaucracy of the Other America
that can't see you
or sees you as something they can't feel
or sees you as an opportunity
to whitewash
or privatize

but there are others, not many
and their spirit is strong

stronger than all the others put together

and they have dug up from the wreckage
a cache of magic instruments:
rusty trumpets
bent trombones
cracked cymbals
dancing shoes
with holes to let the souls in

and they have begun to play these battered
instruments

and they have begun to dance

and their notes drift higher than the clouds
to the drumbeat of ancestral rhythms

and like mist from the bayou
a song of hope rises up
waiting to be heard.

wake up

it will take waves
lapping at doors

it will take wild winds
blowing trees through windows

it will take basements
filled like swimming pools

it will take whole houses
crushed like toothpicks

it will take tidal waves
and plagues
heat waves and starvation

it will take total deprivation

before people wake up
and ask, what happened?

and even then
they won't ask
unless it happens
specifically
to them.

the last wave for my city

it's the last wave for my dying city
and I'm riding it

running out of time to turn the tide
to make the dry rot subside
or watch it take over

the tipping walls
and caving roofs
with sliding shingles
that leave black eyes open
to blue skies
like empty cups to drink pouring rain

and I can hear the slate slip and slap down
and see the shards splinter to the ground
returning to earth

and the plywood pounded
over windows no more
and the phantom factories
with workers no more
and for each fallen porch
and broken stairway to nowhere
you see nature taking over
engulfing
reclaiming what was hers

the crunch of broken bricks
like red crumbs beneath my feet
reminds me that time waits, patient
and relentless

to have lived a life here
is to hear the whisper of bygone voices
echo through these empty streets

and as I walk alone among old ghost homes
I hear warped wood creak and groan
in the clutch of rusty nails
pulling and popping
giving up
and letting go

and the mist of memory
fades like a brittle picture
slowly vanishing

and every day
is a history less remembered

today, less than yesterday

when there was

but now

there isn't.

Mohawk beginnings

the angel flies down
on a bed of blue herons
set softly on the back of a turtle

its shell spreads to the horizon
as the mantle of a newborn earth

while the seeds of life
float from her fingertips
like little pearl-drop embryos
dropped in mud
dripped from muskrat paws

she chants
and walks the sacred circle
calling forth a world to bloom

two sons conceived
Nature and Progress
carry questions of man's earthly destiny

and then a day comes
when the snake shows itself
bright and beautiful
to entice brother Progress

he stares at the snake
so blinded by beauty
to sacrifice all for its promise

power and fame and fortune
is yours, says the snake
for a price: kill your brother

Nature, becoming
tends to his garden
and thinks about ways to help out
impervious to the serpent's enticement
when it offers the same deal to him

the mother approaches the snake
reproaching and warning away
says we are the people with good minds
the keepers of fire and faith

we respect the Creator
and respect all of life
in peace and harmony and balance

so take your temptation
and take your conversions
we don't need your cold blood
or gold chalice

we don't believe in your version of being
our dreams have shown better ways
our progress is brother to nature's becoming
a world quite unlike what you say

so the snakes turns to leave
but then spins with fanged smile
and says, okay... I'll leave for today
but I will return
and the bargain still stands
and eventually
you'll see things my way.

the prism of history

I walked across the street to the museum
and asked: "which way to the industrial history
display?"

"right this way," said the curator
then she led me to a room filled with pictures
and manikin mockups posed like mill workers
toiling away without complaint

I asked, "do you have a section on socialists?"
"socialites? why they're right over here..."
so she showed me the display highlighting
the captains of industry

"no, I said socialists, not socialites!"

"oh, them... uh... well... no... we... um...
don't have anything like that."

"do you know about the Knights of Labor
or the Wobblies...
the ones they called anarchists?
they were here too...
demanding fair pay
a shorter day
some little say about human dignity."

she said, "oh..."
so I asked, "how come your whole story looks
so one-sided?
how come only stories about rich capitalists
and compliant workers?
where's your tribute to the labor leaders
and justice seekers...
the ones who stood up and fought
and got their asses kicked
just so the next generation could have it better...
don't you think they should be given a little credit...
a brief mention?"

she said, "I might bring that up at the next board
meeting."

opposite day

there is a code
to the language they use
a way through the fog toward the meaning

it's discovered by looking at outcomes
to contrast cold facts with deceiving

listen to all the slogans they sling
to uncover their secret intentions
and take the words
and turn them around
to reverse the purpose they mention

such as clear sky initiatives
that darken the air
with soot and particulate matter

or when promised that no child is left behind
but look down, there are no rungs on their ladder

the Patriot Act
makes patriots traitors
and freedom means tapping your phone

free markets mean
the fix is in
and subsidies soon will be flowing

the Clean Water Act
is the right to pollute
and smart growth
means highways and sprawl

and justice means
that rights are intact
for money and power, that's all

while mission accomplished
is perpetual war
and the right to life means dying

and affordable housing
means interest rates floating
sky high with a foreclosure pending

so whatever they say
in the court of the king
just know it's opposite day

where the words that they use
are not what they mean
and the truth is
a game that they play.

tree hugger

big blossoms from the earth
the trees stand majestic

hives of birds chirping songs
dropping turds to seed the soil of life

and the wind carries the cries
and the bees spread the pollen
fruitful to multiply

the bright bursts of color in fall
a last gorgeous sigh before dying

but a rebirth again in-
finite spring times, or until
the axe of fate chops it down

death prematurely ordained
like a saw on call
to some lazy landlord
who sees trees as simply something
they pay to rake up

and the buzz kills my buzz
so I go to the window
and watch the stump grinder finish the job
ripping the roots
falling another filter
another bird house
another shade-tree testament
to a living earth

and another failure to see it.

the soft cage

in the sky there are eyes
that you can't see

they are always watching

these eyes are connected to
other eyes:
a network of judgments

some you can see
like the street cameras
which recognize your face
and turn you into a math equation
run against the database of your history

if you use the internet
they know all about it
what you see
and what you tell

if you use a GPS
or E-ZPass
then they know
the places you go

if you use a cell phone
then they know who you talk to
and what you say
and where you are when you say it

if you use a credit card
then they know the details
of every transaction
and your banking
and your health history
and all the other footprints
of your digital trail
linked
analyzed
and categorized
in secret surveillance
to anticipate the crimes
you might commit

so watch what you do
watch what you say
watch what you post
watch what you watch
watch who you associate with
even watch what you think
because they are working on watching that too.

gazing at your navel

she starts each day
by looking in the mirror:
turns on the computer
and goes straight to her page

it's her digital profile
her new embodiment
her system of self-esteem

it is here
in this ether-world
of video links
posts and pictures
where she feels truly alive

where each day
is a new fifteen minutes
where each new friend
is a tally of her popularity
each trivial comment
a profound inner statement
and each dis or putdown
an invitation to suicide

it is here
out in cyberspace
where she can test her sexuality
exposing secret desires
posing as a porn star

it is here where
she's an actress
playing any part she pleases
invoking personalities
to fit each circumstance

and it is here that
she leaves a trail of indiscretion
that will never disappear
that will follow her
toward every future job prospect
like a tattoo on the neck

so off and on
all through the day
she checks and checks and checks
signing in
to assure herself
for sure, she's somebody special.

a day in the life

the Fed chairman says the outlook is grim:
falling stocks
rising costs
housing crisis
fuel crisis

the cost of gas
through the roof
the cost of food
through the roof
the cost of everything
through the roof
higher and higher
like an empty tank of gas
evaporating into the clouds

the Iraqi puppet
with shrapnel eyes
says everything is going well
despite the anarchy
the civil war
the terrorists
the bombings
the refugees
and the futility

the Pentagon is asking for more money
and they promise to investigate
the overruns, fraud
and unaccounted millions

in Kenya they celebrate democracy
with murder and riots
while in Israel, they plan for peace
by invading Gaza
and building West Bank settlements

police have found bones
buried under the children's home
and the SPCA says
the abused animals are doing fine

the report says
one of every 99 Americans is behind bars
while a shopping mall explosion injures eight

on the political front
the presidential candidates
are breaking all spending records
while the speaker of the house
is demanding a grand jury probe
of the president's staff

safety officials are recalling cribs
which they think are killing babies
and scientists have discovered that
snowflakes are filled with bacteria

at the local level
there is a conference
on saving farms from subdivisions
and another on
how to stop all the floods

and then it's just your everyday assaults
robberies and murders

for good news
the baby abandoned in the taxi is okay
but they can't locate the parents
and the mother
who spent 13 years in prison for her daughter's murder
has been cleared through DNA

meanwhile, in sports news
there's so much cheating
they're talking about asterisks for half the records

on the editorial page
there are two letters—
one says to stop disparaging America
it's the world's greatest country
love it or leave it
and the other says
humans are slowly destroying the planet

just a day in the life of the world
at the end of February in 2008.

bankrupt

welcome to the land of more
where we never have enough

it's a place of enchanted images
dangled from a screen
insatiable needs
manufactured to entice
youth, fame and fortune
sweet beauty for a price

there's a dream house
that should be yours
and a fancy car to envy

there's a trophy wife
with big fake boobs
and sugar daddy spending

there's the neighbors talking
and you hope they wish
they were you
all trying to top each other
in the race for something new

and if you can't afford it
you can borrow
and pay tomorrow

and if the debt is crushing
and the repo man is calling

and if the power
has been shut off
and you just feel like bawling

don't you worry
you're not alone
in the land of not enough
where all the best consumers
of my generation
have gone bankrupt.

contestants of reality

it's in plain sight
but the people don't see it

yet they watch and they watch and
every night they flip the switch
laughing and snickering
at humiliation and disgrace

performing fools
performing for fools
picking sides
setting one against the other
not voting in elections
yet voting for trivia

stuffing their brains with empty calories
knowledgeable about nonsense:
this contestant or that
this scandal or that
put on public display

the cheap indiscretions
crying and fighting
cheating and lying for entertainment
copping reality with planned perversity

how long will it be
before we get to watch
public executions
staged as contests?
with the home-viewing public
in mock participation
pulling the trigger on
some abortion doctor
or sex offender
or faggot?

maybe they'll call it the new education
priming future soldiers
getting them used to the taste of blood

if you try to talk sensible civics
in these channel-flipping days
you confront curt circumventions
and empty slogans
echoed from the hate mongers
and passed on as confused knowledge

but if you ask people
which contestant do you like?
oh, they can tell you so much—
they opine and declaim
express and profess
such detailed expositions about
the contestants in their reality.

wild

a clenched talon in the grip of hunger

sharp teeth to tear hides and sever limbs

the skins that change color and
the background where coats blend in

the poison to kill
the strength to destroy
the speed to catch or evade

stealth cunning to lie in waiting to
pounce then devour their unwary prey

the web of emergent relationships
from swamps to the cities of today

the brains of the highest order
who fashion the world
to conform to their ways

they can see both sides of a coin
and they claim the image of God

they know about eat or be eaten
and they talk about getting along

yet they divide themselves
into groups and sects
and set up a world of divisions

they can't figure out
how to make it all work
lacking eyes with sustainable visions

caught up in the game
competing for fame
and grasping to snag every nickel

fucking and fighting
like animals
and veering us all toward extinction.

I am

I am adrift
in a world of wonder
even in tragedy
I find love

I am lost
on a straight path
but in the web of crossroads
the fork is my comfort

I am standing
strong bodied
learning strength
without it
learning to accept
time

I am a vessel
for ancient gods
who call rhythms
through my hands

I am a voice
of warm unreason
a contrarian
to cold logic

I am a mirror
to my society
reflecting shadows
to give them light

I am a branch
on the oak of the world
dropping acorns
and scattering red leaves

I am a patriot
wearing wolf's clothes
howling cries of freedom
from a hill with no flag

I am a son, a brother
a father, a lover
a neighbor
and citizen of the world

I am a connoisseur
of chaos
peddling conceptual
contemplations

I am a manipulator
of signs and symbols
sending smoke signals
to singe your soul

I fling love notes
from rooftops
like postcards
from paradise lost

I am searching
for sensitive visions
seeking salvation
without religion

I am a teacher
of subversive logic
painting pictures
with indelible ink

I am a star
among a gazillion galaxies
burning bright
and already dead

and if there's a reason
for stars
please tell me
so I know
the reason
I am.

sometimes

sometimes we hold hands
and walk in the moonlight

sometimes
we smooth out all the wrinkles
with smiles
and soft tones

sometimes
when we embrace
all the troubles of the world
seem to drift away
like mist after fallen rain

and sometimes
we invoke magic secrets
with the sensation of our skin

but there are other times
when you can hear the plaster crack
and glass shatter

when nails on blackboards
replace sweet melodies

when a slammed door says, goodbye
and a look of hatred says too much
and the icicles on the cold shoulder
hang like sharp daggers of doubt
ready to break off
and pierce all hope

but most times
they just melt away...
languid pools waiting their turn
to become new icicles
or new mists of love.

desire

they look so sexy
in the underwear magazines
so sultry in their pouty stares

smiling and beaming
pulling up their hair
jutting out their asses
for you to savor

laying it out explicit
saying, wouldn't you like
a piece of this?

so young and perfect
the impossible ideal
airbrushed like dreams of desire

but do you, the men out there
meet women like this?

or does your wife
look like
one of them?

or maybe your daughter
ready to set loose
is posting like poses
on MySpace?

or if you happen to see one
strutting down Broadway
in cold blood
acting too cool to care

do they look at you
pouting and waving love pussy
so ready
just like in the catalogs?

or do they keep walking
and blowing you off
with the dream
and the pose
of desire?

good poems

I predict a great renaissance of poetry:
a coming back and a big leap forward

golden treasure keys
discovered in the sands of time
to open new vistas

dropped down
like celestial seeds
to blossom the essence
just right

like a vitamin, chock full

like a ring you can put right on

attuned to our fragmentation
short on time
short on spirit
short on everything
but need

in sync with the silicon age
of instant gratification
without moment for long-windedness
or relationships

so goodbye, novel
you're just too much commitment
too much strain on my computer eyes

we want it fast and easy
in sound-bite virtual time

but the new poem must be
trickier than slick propaganda
and more cunning than any sales pitch flicker

no empty calories to add new noise

but urgent insurgent secrets to sneak inside
acting easy
wrapped like colored candy
but filled with multitudes
and a profound taste, bitter or sweet
to inspire, ever remembered
and at best, to affect
forever.

witness to the ticking clock

they document the world's contours
in simplified space
telling us where

once by hand
now coded in fast double digits

they are witness to the ticking clock:
a bird's eye view of the cliff's edge

they demarcate the material:
the growing footprint
like a spreading fungus across the landscape

they conjure the unseen in themes
of social strata made manifest
the bright color demographics of our inequality

they can see with eyes from space
which reflect back our misdirection
in numbered squares

and they link disparate data
to connect the dots of pending tragedies
like species loss
like climate change
like resource depletion

and these simplified pictures of a changing world
reveal a complexity otherwise unseen:
the web of life's relationships taken for granted

and if maps are power
then every updated atlas
is a record of our power to destroy
and our powerlessness to reverse course

yet up on the clouds the mapmakers stand
with rainbow legends to illuminate
to foster understanding of the big picture
trying to move us beyond the looking.

the good planners

I'm not a good planner
because I don't like rules
or follow them very well
and urban planning
is mostly about rules

I'm not a good planner
because I don't play politics
and don't belong to a party
and urban planning is mostly
about politics

I'm not a good planner
because I don't believe in
the status quo
and planning is mostly
about preserving it

I'm not a good planner
because I don't believe in
objectifying life with numbers
but planning is mostly
about traffic counts
and sales receipts

I'm not a good planner
because I don't fetishize growth
but planning is all about promoting it

I'm not a good planner
because suburban sprawl is the norm
yet I'm a lover of cities

I'm not a good planner
because my eyes see the future
but NIMBYs have no need
for vision

I'm not a good planner
because I like to walk and bike
but planning is mostly about cars

I'm not a good planner
because I speak my mind
yet good planners sit quiet
and follow the program

I'm not a good planner
because I'm uncertified
and my library is not in their study guide

I'm not a good planner
because I'm not satisfied with slogans
and weary methods that don't work
yet planning is all about sound bites
and failed policies

I'm not a good planner
but there are some people
who tell me I am
but I tell them, no
I'm not a good planner.

the forest and the trees

there are people
who are the most proficient bureaucrats

they know all the ropes, rules, and regulations

they are actually quite smart in this way, with
so many details to master

gray skin and squinting eyes
they dwell within cubicles
spending dry days dotting i's
without any conception of scale

writing bleached words no one reads
acronyms of confusion
encrusted in codes
substituting standards for freedom
substituting procedures for thinking
waving rulebooks to pirate authority

Kafka, dizzy with despair
dreamed nightmares in the bureaucratic maze—
his art, like all art, too sincere for red tape

the vertiginous incongruity
between the details
and the big picture
as bland bullets
replace warm words
in a machine language
molding mass minds

rule breakers
category jumpers
and vision seekers
know instinctively that
if you crave understanding
you will fail
unfulfilled
if you only draw conclusions
through one eye
scientifically
in minute detail
with bureaucratic blinkers on

the world of man is no
simple science
to dwell within cells
or bait bacteria
for breakthroughs

cells make a body
a part of the whole
like people, the cells of society

understood by the distance
of a collective scale
in a perspective of
organized complexity
higher patterns emerge
for those with open minds

so step back all you paper pushers
and red-tape peddlers

step back all you sound-bite specialists
marketing simplicity
selling stupidity

step back all you narcissists
thinking it's only about you

and we the people:
wipe the minutiae from your eyes!
unbrainwash yourselves!
wrap your arms around time
and uncertainty
and openness to a change of perspective
so we can connect the subjective dream dots
that make our forest out of trees.

they talk

they meet every month
and they talk

they talk about streams
and water quality

they talk about collecting data
and forming coalitions

they talk about advocacy
and change

they talk about all the ways
that we stumble and bumble
making a mess as we go:
dead fish
pesticide poison
heavy metals
PCBs
habitat loss
deforestation
stream degradation...

they talk about how
we must do things differently

they care
and they talk and they talk

but they are not empowered
to effect change
to influence the decision makers
to do things differently

so they just talk.

knowledge

still winds in the heart
while waiting in wonder

not knowing what
or why

silent signatures
to messages
never quite clear

a pleading with oneself
to feel okay
in the day of surprises

behind the gray coating
in hidden blue sunlight
there is a cycle
and a secret system
build on god-like knowledge

so we must become god-like
to fully understand.

today

today is the day
to change the world

I will get up early
drink strong coffee
do a million push-ups
and read every book in my library

preparation for the big event

I will fix my children
a big spread breakfast
and read them the paper out loud
not to scare, but to prepare
to brace for what they'll face

I'll tell them, with love
you are the warriors of the future
it's up to you to finish
that which I cannot

and today's the day
when I will make every delayed phone call
and write letters to all my friends

I will tell them all
that time is short
we have to act now or never

I will run around and brandish petitions
get everyone to sign them
and I will take them to the protest
then I'll nail them to my congressman's door

today is the day
when I'll write a big book
to change the consciousness of my time

and I will fill my notebooks
with poetry
that soars like eagles in flight

and today's the day
when I'll make a big speech
and pour out all my passion

and today I'll show up for work early
and be the last one to leave

and today is the day
when I will say
to everyone, I'm sorry

and today's the day
when I'll invent
a cure for sick confusion

and today's the day
I give everything away
and volunteer
down at the soup kitchen

and today's the day
when I'll call up
the president
and say
stop the bullshit, man
you're fucking up the world!

today's the day.

family friendly

they told her the job was
family friendly
and since she had a family
friendly sounded swell

so she quit the old job
which was kind of unfriendly
and started the family friendly one

then they lowered the boom:
you must drive out-of-state
for day-long meetings
up early, and home late

you must work weekends and nights

you must work harder
to meet your quota

you must give to the company

they made her mouth
start chewing on her fingers
gnawing nails down to stubs

they made her stomach
knot up tight like a cramp

they made her resent
her husband, who didn't have
a family friendly job like hers

they made flames
shoot out of her mouth
at the slightest disagreement

they made her talk to counselors
who sat quiet and dreamt of
getting in her pants

they made her pour glass upon glass
when she got home each day

and then one day
they cut her pay
and told her they wanted more

and she said
I've given you all I can
what more do you want?

here... take my family!

the richest nation
in the world

they've closed all the madhouses
and shuttered the treatment centers

sent out into the world
like tweety birds knocked from the nest

they wake with damp dew on cracked faces
and piss stains dampen their dirty pants

their morning song is a mumble, a murmur
of pain through missing teeth

they shuffle and stumble, broken winged
and pull worm butts from the ground to light up

slumped piles sprawling against walls
with withered hands
and rheumy-eyed pleas for spare change

ignored
spit at
scowled at
scuffed waste of the world

told you can't
told you must
told to move on
and stop making people nervous
with your filth and misery

can't you just...
why don't you find a...
sorry but you'll just have to...

Santa's new neighbor

they've dug a big cave
in a glacier in Norway
not far from the North Pole

inside they hope to protect
millions of crops
from the ravages of war
natural disasters
and climate change

a global seed vault as
insurance policy, they hope
like Noah's Ark
containing the biological diversity
of the planet

they're being farsighted
thinking ahead
concerned about future generations

they can see what's coming
and it doesn't look good
so they're preparing for the worst

it's built way down
under a frozen mountain
and fashioned to withstand nuclear attack

can you imagine
some war monger of the future
set to blow up the world
and thinking, "wait... what about those seeds?
how dare they think they will eat tomatoes some day...
nuke it!"

at a cost of only nine million dollars
extra air conditioning units and all
they see it as a real bargain
for one thousand years of potential rebirth

and think how happy
the mutant survivors will be
when they find out about the seeds

and if they don't have any way to get them
assuming the airlines have cancelled flights
indefinitely
they can always ask for seeds for Christmas

just tell Santa:
I've been a good survivor all year
I haven't looted or murdered
or eaten any of my neighbors
and since you're right in the neighborhood
could you swing by
and pick me up some seeds for Christmas?

there must be something up there
that can grow in radioactive ash?

if not, could you bring me
some of those poppy seeds from Afghanistan?
I'm sick of the smell of death
and need a ticket to a new world.

the host and the parasite

he stands in front of the audience
and shows them slides:
maps, facts and pictures
of sprawl

he shows them landscapes
and points out the shortcomings:
the disconnectedness
the lack of sidewalks
the spread-out auto-dependency

he talks about progress as a question:
the unintended consequences
the waste and abandonment
where escape is sold as advancement
and segregation the ideal

and he challenges bad policies:
the subsidies and inducements
the onerous regulations
that zone out sustainable urbanism

and he outlines a future
where oil runs out
while its wastes
overheat a sick planet

then he puts down the mirror
and takes questions from furrowed brows
but none come

the next speaker is introduced

he too shows slides:
bullet points and paragraphs
containing words such as growth
infrastructure
and economic development
which he reads to them verbatim

and when he invokes the landscape
he sees big boxes
big parking lots
big signs
and big bulldozers
which make him smile

he puffs out his chest
sucks in his gut
and talks about jobs
and low taxes

but he doesn't say anything about
low wages or poor benefits
or how chain stores ship out the profits
and kill mom and pops

he doesn't say anything about
traffic, smog, or stormwater either

and he doesn't mention anything about
the city next door, or
their desolate downtown
vacant buildings
and high taxes
though he needs their water
and their customers to make his schemes fly

he doesn't criticize the sprawl at all

he sees it as progress, an aspiration

and the audience
like minded
with no lost love for cities
blinked and nodded
and asked a few questions
about traffic and taxes
and were reassured that
more sprawl would solve both

you could hear them talking as they left:
they didn't like that first speaker
making them uncomfortable with his criticism
exposing their wrinkles with his mirror

but they liked the second one:
he made them feel good about themselves
telling them they would all live
happily ever after
in the sprawl.

American psychos

there was another shooting yesterday
with seven dead this time
on a college campus like last year

another random psycho snapping
blasting innocents
then blasting himself

it's been happening a lot lately
have you noticed?

last week it was a shopping mall
happy consumers taken out Rambo style
the ultimate purchase, your life

shopping malls and schools
the preferred backdrop
for video game reenactment
live, in meat space

and how about the kid who hacked his parents?
and the brother who hacked his sister?
and the father who hacked the mother?

why all the hacking and blasting?

seems it's always some loner
male, black coat
armed to the teeth
likes horror movies
and video games, comics
and TV
but doesn't like people
and doesn't like himself

and how about the pampered teenagers
who light homeless people on fire
or beat some helpless stranger
and film it for the world to see?

or the sad sad soldiers
on break from defending freedom
who come home to suicide
or to shoot their wives in the head?

or the aspiring gangster
who must kill a stranger to join the club?

blood is in every solution

is this the logical terminus of consumerism?
virtualized
desensitized
looking for kicks
and programmed for violence?

oh, the people will talk

they'll talk about heightened security
cameras
metal detectors

they'll talk about bad parents
counseling
and drug therapy

and some will even talk about
the media
and our glorification of
sex, brutality
and materialism

but the competing experts
shout sound bites at deaf ears
one says this, the other says that
canceling each other out
until no one hears
no one understands
and no one cares

then we'll fall back into our routine
here in America:
worrying about terrorists
worrying about immigrants
worrying about some random foreign boogeyman
from some far away place
invading the sanctity of our American paradise
trying to cause us harm.

have a nice day

there might be days when
you want to give the whole world
the finger

when your asshole neighbor
driving on your grass
making all that noise
leaving all that mess
deserves the bird, not a wave
but don't do it

there might be days when
that grinding commute
that cut-me-off jackass
that escalating fill 'er up
make you want to
jump right off the bridge
but don't do it

there might be days when
that dreary parking lot
that dreary cubicle
and the dreary drudgery
of your daily paper push
make you want to
tell your boss where to stuff it
but don't do it

and there might weeks and weeks
when it seems like nothing but
dark clouds and cold rain

when everyone you count on
is sticking it in your back

when you feel like
you're all alone in this wide world
which makes you want to leave it
but don't do it

because somewhere
behind all the bullshit
is a sunny day
a good time
a kind word
a decent break
a tasty morsel
a warm body
and a sweet smile
somewhere

so have a nice day.

economic development

they dumped a big pile of cash on the table
and said, "here, have some free market"
then they laughed

they told the public it was about jobs
and leveling the global playing field

they have friends in construction
all set to take a nice slice
and kick back some

they strike a giveaway deal
with a big multi-national
promising big buildings
big infrastructure
big jobs

they grant tax breaks
and outright cash
the public purse pried open
and millions dumped on the table
so much
some dropped on the floor
and they just looked at it
and laughed
and lit up cigars
smiling.

lines

a small patch of forest
sliced, stacked and carted off:
the Lincoln Logs of blueprint dreams

neatly piled
like slaves or sardines
the straight-line logic
of product and profit

the lineage of ledger lines
as fence posts
as subdivisions
as coffins

like lines at the checkout counter
the turnstile
the fire escape

like lines of commuter cars
dreaming of the fast lane
retirement
or salvation

there are lines of downtrodden
claiming welfare and food stamps
and lines of loud cattle cars
despairing of hamburger

hopeless the lines
in the mess halls of prisons
and hopeful the greased lines
of lobbyists in Washington

there are lines to take sacraments
while waiting for heaven
and lines behind Virgil
down flight to damnation

everywhere, there are lines—

the lines of the train track
the jet plane
the power poles

the stream lines
of river-dumped
stormwater pipes

the lines of the crackhead
with rolled dollar waiting

the lines of the lemmings
with leaders deceiving

and the long lonely-line cadence
of soldiers marching
in endless waves
off to trade freedom
for Arlington graves.

plastic

I saw the credit card bill
sticking out of her purse
and I couldn't help but look

holy shit!
she's racked up a hell of a goddamn bill!

I felt like a lizard
with one eye locking on the finance charges
and the other on the late fees and overcharges

and there was another bill
so I looked at that too
what the...!

now I have a problem

she's been crying about her cut in commission
how she's broke
can't pay bills right now

but apparently this hasn't stopped
the spending:
Victoria's Secret
Macy's
Banana Republic
$100 dollar jeans...

now she's dug a hole so deep
she can't get out

and didn't bother to tell me

so now it is me
who has to climb in that hole
and pull her out...
me, the one who didn't splurge and spend
in the world of financial reality
but now must
drain scrimped savings
to save her ass

and help pay the interest
on all that fancy stuff
she can't afford
but bought so easy
with plastic

so I help her develop a new payment plan
with background music
that sounds like scissors cutting:
snipping Visa
snapping Master
clipping plastic into the pail.

get in front of the troops

the bumper sticker said:
if you're not behind the troops
you can get in front of them

and I thought, well...
there you go
another numbskull with
his hatred redirected at me

I'm against the war that he supports
and have been all along

but I have yet to meet
one person
out of all the people against the war
not one person
who doesn't support the troops

if anything, the troops are
the ones everyone feels worst about
getting maimed and killed
shell-shocked and fucked up for what?

forced to blow apart innocent people
who hate us now more than ever
helping recruit future terrorists
perpetuating our military plans

what I'm against can be boiled down to
two groups, neither one
the troops

the first are the payroll politicians
who started and support this mess
and the second are
the jackass Americans who support them
and display their ignorance on their bumpers

what I really wish is that
they were the ones, these
two groups...
they were the ones sent to fight
and die in the folly of their own making.

the nest

to grow up in one house

to spend your whole childhood
in one place, one house
is to become part of that house, it
part of you
forever

I can see the porch and remember
all those days up there
playing, dreaming
talking, reading
looking out
at the world passing by

I can see myself as a child on the sidewalk
meting out torture with a magnifying glass
playing army men
cowboys and Indians
or hide and seek
with my brothers and friends

and riding my bike down the street
to the flip-flap
of clothespinned cards on spokes

or the time a bird let loose on my hand
as I rode by, and in the car later
I repeated a word I heard on the corner
fucking bird... fucking bird...
and my mother said, "what!"

I remember the World War II vet
who'd limp by each day
and give me gum and baseball cards

and the close-knit neighborhood
of single- and two-family houses
elbow to elbow
and the little nearby shops:
the corner grocery
the confectionaries with candy, ice cream, magazines
the pizzeria with a game room and juke box
and the ball fields at the opposite end of the block
near my old school

and when I think about my childhood home
it's as if a third parent has shaped me
melding my sense of space and security
like the second womb of my awakening

but now there are strangers living there
with their lives being shaped
by the same benevolent force
that shaped my family
and I hope it is as good to them
as it was to us

and last night, I was reminded of my old house
by a recurring dream that took place out front:

a shadow flew down from the maple tree
and me the young boy stood listening
as it whispered its secret message in my ear
fluttering next to my head it said...
then flew up high and I flew with it
higher and higher
like hawks to the sun
with two messages:
one to tell
and one to keep secret
forever.

ballerina

a soft knock on the door

little feet beneath my desk

she says, "hi Daddy"
with big bubblegum eyes
that connect with mine
as I reach out my hands to lift her

"what are you doing Daddy?" she asks
"writing," I say
a story for you:
a story about butterflies
and ballerinas
and baby dolls...
and there's a beautiful princess
who wears pretty dresses
and ice skates
and sings

and when she dances
angels join her
and lift her up like she's flying

and she laughs.

ghosts

"what are those?" she asked, as we drove past

"gravestones"

"what are gravestones?"

oh boy, I thought...

"um... that's where people get buried when they die"

"what's die?"

"a... that's what... a... I don't know, really...
when your body doesn't work anymore"

she's only four

she starts to cry
"I don't want to go down in the ground!"

"don't cry honey... it's okay..."

but I'm not sure what else to say...
do I tell her a tale
and which one?

tell her people go to heaven
and then try explaining what that is?

or tell her people are born again
as cows or birds?

or do I tell her we just die
and that's it?

sometimes parents don't have
all the answers.

fishing

they sit hiding
with guns pointed
and engines running

their game is a numbers game
to meet quotas
and generate revenue

and just below the unstated surface
is a second game called:
profiles for a fishing expedition

the rules depend on who's watching

the contestants wear a coat of dark skin

and the goal of the game is to stop and shakedown

to search for a pipe or the smell of a roach
or if lucky some bricks in the trunk
or the smell of some booze
or a warrant outstanding
or forged green cards and bad luck

the consolation prize
a pink ticket
for speeding just like they all do
or if they think you're a hottie, maybe
they'll let you on through for a screw

so every day the game is played
pointing their guns at me
yet I know where they hide
and I've nothing to hide
and as soon as I'm past them I speed.

the stream of consciousness

have you seen people talking to themselves?

I see it all the time:
mostly people in cars
or walking down the street
though mostly in cars
since most people drive these days

sometimes they're quite animated
waving their hands
shaking their heads
carrying on a conversation
or argument
full voice
no mere mumble
and no headset either
(though sometimes you see that too)

it looks funny
so when I see them talking solo, I laugh

but if they see you laugh, they stop
not wanting to appear crazy, I suppose
which is the common assumption, that
anyone who talks out loud to themselves
must be crazy

yet I've caught myself doing it too

and how about you?

maybe we're all a little nuts?

how much?

they can put a price tag on anything
turn anything into a commodity

like land
which the aborigines everywhere
saw as sacred, communal
unownable
yet we the people
from the land of capitalism
turn it into a primary aspiration:
we claim it
fight over it
seize it
parcel it
market it
position it to ring gold coins
with the right patronism
subsidies
and infrastructure

we put a price tag on water
we put a price tag on pollution

we sell our bodies
our labor
our souls

we assign values to victims
we cost claim hurricanes
and everything, baby, has its price

cost benefit analysis
will analyze for you
whether your tax bill
or health care can endure it

they put a price tag on access
to take certain highways

they tag a worthiness value to you

they have even priced out the cost of a life
and they're working on the entry fee to heaven

everything, friends
has a price tag to pay
and there aren't any specials today.

peace of mind

like dark clouds
on the edge of your horizon
always there
threatening rain

hiding just beyond your ear, sometimes
reaching around with black claws
to scratch clarity from your eyes

even when everything seems perfect
it peeks in your window
just to remind you
it's still there

elusive, yet omnipresent
it shape-shifts into many forms

it is the bills unpaid
the lover unfaithful
the pink slip
slipped in your inbox

it is gas prices rising
new wars started
the climate cooking new furies

it is the stock market falling
the housing bubble bursting
the economy swirling flushed down

it is the smog in the sky
the lead in the paint
the mercury in the fish you can't eat

it is the election returns
the final test score
the acceptance letter never accepted

it is the child being born
the daughter on a date
the son sent away to fight wars

it is the roof leaking rain
the furnace on fire
the flood that is filling your basement

and sometimes
you can't even name it
but it's there, lurking
always jerking your mind
jarring your slumber
taunting you like an itch you can't scratch

whispering wisps of worry to wear your weary soul
thin.

the man and his wife

the truck was parked
jutting into my driveway
making it hard for me to back out

I said, "excuse me... you're not planning on parking..."
but I stopped when I saw the mattress get heaved on
the truck

"moving out already?" I asked

he turned and stuck out his hand to shake and said
"well... it's like this..."
then he told me about her death:
"thirty-six years we were married!
sixty-one is pretty old to be starting over!"

He said he lost the house, the job
just about everything
because of her

he saw her face everywhere
her walk and whisper
her shoes
her jewelry and lotions
panties and bras...

he saw the lipstick smear on the tie
that he forgot to dry-clean...

that's what got him good, the lipstick smear
it made him mad with remembrance of
every suck smile lip lap and lust lunge

and it sent him packing
moving with the wind now
floating old and aimless

I wished him well

I couldn't tell if he was gonna make it.

the wall between wills

I make a plea, a supplication
for a personal point of view

you seem to listen, a little
to hear, and not hear

there is a barrier between us
a fortification of will
a stubborn doing anyway

being ignored sends echoes
of a loud yell and
red-faced stammers
demanding reasons

the barrier grows

a repetition recalls a familiar reception:
the half ear, half eye dissonance
already filed before finished
with my words
an imperfect fit
with your hearing's understanding

in agreement's asking
there is weak confirmation
and unstated incongruity

it is a weariness

with enough stamina
to override
at the first opportunity
of my unknowing

it is a test of wills
and a wall between them
built on choices
to add new bricks
or to take some away.

the spirit to suffer

the Old World spirit lived on
in the children of the new America

born from soul-searching Europeans
with bent backs and peasant hands
who caught a glimpse of the shining western star
gleaming from across the Atlantic that said, come...

these children of the new America
had not yet learned about wanting everything
were not yet molded
by the myth of something for nothing

a penny was a penny
it had value not to squander:
there was blood and sweat in that copper toil
so you cherished it

these children of the new America
were ready when the crash came:
they already knew fifteen ways to make potatoes
how a stitch in time made perishing pant knees persist
or that popped button sewn with patient fingers
rocking, humming hymns
patching many more miles into sad-soul shoes
to walk downtrodden paths to jobs for pennies
and be glad

it was a stoutness of spirit
a proud independence
it said, I'm here
and I can walk among trash barrels
and still be clean

I can make practically nothing
and still save for rainy days

I can endure suffering
because it is a suffering
incomparable to the suffering
that brought me here

this is the spirit of my grandmother
a Polish beauty of independence:

the woman who saw in the slick suave darkness
of my Italian grandfather, a movie-star figure
with no movie credits:
a sharp-suited hipster
with a swagger and a smile
and the penetrating eyes of a Latin lover
that swept her off her feet

swept the child of a grocer into his arms
into a marriage with two daughters
into a web of sisters by marriage
who still waited on, pampered
doted on their little brother
reinforcing his spoiled male role
laying expectations at his feet
for his new wife to follow

but she had expectations too:
the paycheck brought home
with a clear-eyed kiss
not empty handed
rheumy eyed
loaded, sneery smile
of after-work bar bender

that Polish tongue
sharp when taunted
let lash the fury
of pent up Old World frustrations
pushing away the man
with no spirit for confrontation
to run to his sisters for cover
or back to the bar

the young girls of this mother
one my mother
learned harsh lessons about love
and booze and big broken promises

so when their time came
they chose carefully
hoping to avoid a lifetime of suffering

because these children of
the children of the new America
had less of that Old World blood
were less fortified against heartbreak
without diaspora or depression in their memory
and so softer in a world of prosperity and expectations

but it was the Old World stoutness
that sustained their mother:
the strength to endure so low loneliness
to never remarry
to live alone in orderly solitude
to never drive but make do
fifty-odd years like a nun in this world

sustained by bent fingers
and stubbornness
scrimped savings
and a small stipend

her beautiful features, she
looked twenty years younger
like her daughters' generation
though nearly one hundred

the little spotless apartment
perfect meals prepared
and no scrap wasted

the slow meticulous chewing
born of isolation
and all the time of a lifetime
to contemplate what was
and what will never be.

the road

I can remember that dreamscape
driving coast to coast
from green mountains
to golden corn plains
to the orange and purple majesties
of four corner visions

the steep decline into Albuquerque
into Denver
up and up Rocky Mountains
and over the long hot yucca moonscape
of Death Valley

six times across this land of fable and myth
six times searching
three times landing in the city of angels
looking for my star on Hollywood Boulevard
but only finding new roads to travel

the crossroads of transition
standing at the abyss looking up
flying over old highways
leading where spirits pull
the blood drips consecrated kisses
humming old songs
and a rhythm forever remembered

I look through shrouded dreams
for amplified meanings
hearing sustained notes of a past forgotten
hearing young voices now turned old
seeing youth in all its naive beauty
full of starry eyes and images
that cloud corrupted cores

the map laid out
in concrete and mortar
printed patterns for later use

the babbled voices
and broken people
without a compass to point them home

and I fill my basket overflowing
packing in every morsel of America
to carry back in locked-box memory
to unpack in later days
to see the sad beauty and last hurrah
the young dream catcher
seeking a destiny
too young to know
it's an apparition
found only in the searching.

the one-gun salute

when I pull myself out of bed
my back and neck and knees creak

those old football injuries
coming back to haunt me
trying to put me in a wheelchair

when I sit reading
my eyes get blurry
and I can feel the furrows widen

maybe I'm going blind
or finally just need glasses?

my wrist aches from years of drumming
and I wonder if it will seize up
like an engine without oil

there is this high-pitched ringing
that never stops
like a drill in my ears
screaming: you should have worn ear plugs

as I sit here writing
my back pops and grinds
like popcorn and rusty hinges

and the dentist says
I'm grinding my teeth
and at night I should wear a mouthpiece

and my doctor says
my blood pressure's high
and someday this might kill me

but until that day
I'll just keep bumping and grinding
hammering away
happy for now
that my muscles are strong
I still have my hair
and my mind is a steel spear
like the one that rises each day
below my waist
and I salute it
for reminding me that
I'm still alive and kicking.

the proud father

he has golden hair like a sunrise
and the mirrors of his blue eyes
reflect me

he takes the bat
steps to the plate
elbows out, back bowed
and cracks one to left field

on first he steals second
second to third
pumps fists
when a hit sends him home

three months later
a little colder
he buckles his helmet
and runs to the huddle

he takes the handoff
bolts forward
cuts left
right
breaks a tackle
to the sideline
and gone!

me, the father
proud as a peacock
cheers like a little kid

then the glance
from the field to the sideline
my ten-year-old gives me
that sidelong look
checking
seeking acknowledgement
confirming in my eyes
my smile
my indescribable satisfaction...

that's my boy!

Popeye

I said, "come on...taste it"
and I put a fork-full of spinach on his plate

"try it...it'll give you big muscles!"

"no! no! I don't like spinach!"

"come on...at least try it once..."

eech! a face, what a face!
then he started gobbling his pasta
without chewing
and guzzling his milk
mad
acting like he's gonna puke

so I got mad too...and yelled

but later I felt bad thinking about yelling
and his crinkled face

I said, "sorry son...didn't mean to yell...
just wanted you to try it"

and he said, "that's okay Dad"
and gave me a big hug

then he showed me his muscles and said
"see...I don't need spinach!"

Bongo

my one and only dog, Bongo
half Great Dane, half pit, was
the best

he looked like he could tear you good, but
in nine years never, not one bite

I took him everywhere and taught him
words like sit and stay, and
he did, until I called

we'd walk and he'd wait
at the corner until the word, okay, he'd
wait outside the store, no leash, until
the word okay, he'd wait
with that big tongue waving, waiting
for my tongue to say okay

walks were ecstasy, and the word walk
sent him crazy running, panting
no need to even say it, just the lead up:
"do you want to go for a..."
and he'd be up wagging, huffing, saying
a walk! fuck yeah, let's go!

he'd whip after the tennis ball, or
stick that I'd fling

and he'd chase me around the house, me
like a little kid running, up
the front stairs, down
the back stairs, him
slipping and sliding, big paws on
wood floors, me
afraid he'd crash, him
whining and running

he was over one hundred pounds and
ran like a charging bull, and
one time he ran right into a chain link fence
full force...knocked back five feet...he got up
shook his head like a stunned fighter, then
ran on like nothing happened

with my baby son he was perfect:
never growled when he climbed
and pulled and tried to ride him
like a little Indian on a horse

but one day it happened, the seizures
out of the blue while I was petting his back
down he went, shaking
foaming at the mouth, me
thinking he's dying
crying his name

he got up stunned, and me
stunned too, not sure what to do

the vet said, "who knows?"
could be this or that or this
but none of it good, and
there was nothing to do

for a month, nothing, then
another, then
another, getting closer together
getting worse

then one morning my
best friend came in my room
and told me...
he nudged me awake, panting
nervous
knowing...
he said, I love you...
let me out to die...goodbye...
and thank you for everything...

so I got up and opened the back door
and he turned, fearful and sad
gave me one final look of love, then lay down
and died

and I just sat there and cried.

okay

I don't want my kids to be force-fed religion

I don't want them to swallow
an interpretation put off as fact

I don't want them to be satisfied
with only one point of view

I want to equip them with
open eyes
open minds
open arms

the ability to discriminate
substance from style
sugar from saccharine

but not:
your melanin content
the accent in your mouth
the length of your hair
the label on your clothes
or the thickness of your wallet

I want to read them
the Bible
the Koran
and all the other big books of myth
we use to talk about mystery

read like literature
not dogma
probing the contradictions of creation
and purpose
of love and hate
passion and power

I want them to know
the four noble truths
and see with Zen minds

I want them to sample, in time
a contemplation of our whole condition

to feel sympathy for all the sorrow and joy
with reasoned understanding

and to drink life like a chocolate milk
with the lick of the lips and a smile
that says: okay.

once upon a time

my little city so full of shadows:
there used to be...
and there once was...
and I remember when...

all along the creek
used to be factories

on every other corner
used to be bars

in every patch of woods
used to be parties

and in so many houses
used to be friends

in every neighborhood
used to be mom and pop shops

and down near the river
used to be a downtown

but not now

nothing now
but old ghosts
and used-to-be's

and the rot of abandonment
everywhere

and in the wind
faint voices
from a faraway time
whispering memories
that only yesterday's ears can hear.

the city of yesterday's
tomorrow

the scene is my little city
bent through the eye of memory
conceived of blood and dreams
at the dawn of a new America

the first came nearly alone
brandishing their sacred book
convinced it was God talking
telling them to spread it

draped in dreary brown
the hooded heads
and the cross they waved
chanting, you are the devil's people
repent! and shun your evil ways
shun the spirits you see in these woods
and see the light in this book!

and the natives struck back
waving their own wood
to tomahawk their priestly scalps
and show them whose god was stronger

and there were sailors and traders
from the land of wooden shoes
hungry with hope, dreaming lush visions
and hardened with the ambition
to turn blood into gold

with winded sails
they floated the salty river of ocean origins
to set up Fort Orange at Albany

they set out on foot
with dried beef and determination
following the western fork
through forests marked with moccasin footprints
filling sacks with trapped beaver
and discovering the land of Eden on its own terms
shorn of the myth in the winds

they heard the woods speak:
the howl of wolves
the cry of the coyote
the roar of the cougar

they saw elk, deer and immense antlered moose;
there were black bears and brown bears
fox and fowl
the sky aflight with big birds of prey

the eagles that soared against the sunrise
and the cry of hawks with snakes
dangling in clutched talons

fish of all stripes leaped up in startled splashes
pulled into canoes by red men they called savages:
the aboriginal dreamers first encountered

from Britain and France
the orders of kings and queens
old greed and disease
old superstitions
bent notions of superiority
and ingrained inclinations toward conquest

they fought and connived
bartered and butchered
negotiated conversions and swindles

and there came a pale-faced chameleon
with an uncle and some land
who became master of exchange and love
with his Irish eyes smiling
he laid out the logistics of land
alliances, and battle plans

he led scalping parties
he led peace treaties
he led proxy wars that led to revolution

and on the dusk of his death
the earth shook with a final upheaval
sending his faithful followers into exile

and when the smoke cleared
and a new flag had been raised
the empty land sat waiting and aching for industry

there was a fast-flowing steam
full of limestone and energy
and a fast-talking industrialist
who was ready to harness the churning
with turbines turning
and the grist of the mills being born

and the wind carried the call of the future
across oceans, to hungry ears, to parched throats
with beaten-up shoes they climbed sad boats
hearing whispered words of hope in the winds of desire

they huddled through Ellis
with nothing but Old World prayers, torn suitcases
and dark eyes looking up in wonder and frightened awe
face to face with the promised land

but big New Amsterdam
was too much for some villagers with peasant hearts
and souls from the soil of proportion

so they went north toward vague contacts, relatives
or nothing more than a railroad stop
with help wanted factories

and one stop was the little village of Veedersburg
which soon claimed the name Amsterdam for itself

the soil of this new world
was trampled by hooves pulling barges
and poked with pounded rail ties
tying the city to the world

the train whistles roared, and said move it!
and the trolley cars rang down Main Street
past little shops stalls and stands
banks and barter houses
clubs and confectionaries
apothecaries
fruit stands
grocers and fishmongers

there were peddlers of new ideas
old dreams
slippery swindles
and gold nuggets

and there was no turning back now
so you made do, hoping the sun
was out there somewhere
ready to shine down on you
and help open some factory door of your future

and you could hear the mumbled prayers on Sunday
the pleading with Old World angels
asking God for guidance
a rent check, or a second chance

unaware that in this land other spirits once dwelled
spirits old as the long-gone longhouse
where the drum chant dream songs of the bear clan
sprang from the turtle-back earth

but now there were new prayers offered
to the god Moloch
where the sacrifice was, everything
and the words were, the whir of machines
and the incense stick was, a smokestack, and
the church was, a factory
and the pews, an assembly line
and the daily offering, your blood sweat and tears
sewing and weaving and assembling
for pennies

and they came:
Irish, Germans
Italians, Poles
Russians...

and made brooms from river hay
and buttons from sea shells
they sewed linens and cottons
and weaved great rugs

there were saloons on every corner, all bellies up
and they would stumble home
dreary-eyed wet whistles
bent back along tenement sidewalks
dreaming of hot soup
and the warm thighs of wifey waiting

and the mystics among them
might look up at the soot-filled panorama
and imagine Paradise and the Inferno
had finally joined hands

they'd see the church steeples and the smokestacks
competing for the attention of the Almighty
framing majestic views of the valley
and the green patchy hillsides
covered with farms like some postcard
or picture in a storybook

and they would dream of the old country
the memories
and people they left behind
and they would cry

and like seditious stowaways
old gripes followed them from Europe:
dissident thoughts and ideas about politics
and utopian notions about sharing

and when the apparition of Marx appeared
passing through on tour of America
they assembled to hear the speeches

there were the Knights of Labor
the IWW, and assorted soapbox socialists
preaching a new kind of religion
called rights and fairness

they rallied with raised fists
and they walked out in solidarity
leading strikes in the streets
demanding justice for the exploited

but there was more solidarity in the lines that waited:
the scab lines full of hungry teeth that said
if not you, me

so history was written
and the agitators were the villains
or simply whitewashed out of the story
no high school lessons about dissent, or how
they wobbled away wounded
asses kicked
tarred and feathered in some places
labeled treasonous subversives
sent packing in cattle cars
dumped in the desert
or shipped off with a one-way ticket
to worship their pagan economics elsewhere
maybe to get shot down in Ludlow
or made the fall guy for a Haymarket riot

but they pushed on anyway
stubborn for justice
dodging vigilante bullets
county sheriffs
state police
and the National Guard
all lined up to do the bidding
of big business

they took pick-axe bludgeons
ducked truncheons
a punch in the face
or just plain shot...
that's what you get

for dreaming of fair pay
and an eight-hour day

so the unearned increment
was pocketed by the wealthy industrialists
who poured exploited blood into the foundations
of their mansions on Guy Park Avenue:
big Victorians full of porches and fireplaces
proud testaments to their station
and proof that progress marched on for some

and on it did, with new inventions made elsewhere:
zippers, vacuums, plastics, synthetics
the rush of modern progress
sent the old industries of Amsterdam
way down south to Dixie
where it was cheaper to break backs
and dump toxic dyes

and it was a dark day when they
pulled the rug over the city's eyes
and the rug city made rugs no more

the people cried
and said goodbye
and moved away to follow the shifting clouds
of the drifting American dream

and those who stayed
learned to live with anger and heartbreak
and the sad sick spirit of decline

as new neighbors came

a day late and a peso short
with shaded skin
and Spanish tongues
they moved in
just in time
to watch the factories close

so the collective cries went out for help
as the disease of deindustrialization
spread throughout the old Northeast

then someone saw dollar signs
so plans were hatched
in the swamps of Washington
to try and fix the cities with
an infusion called Urban Renewal

and the money was spread
around statehouses
and city halls everywhere
backroom plans fashioned
plans to fight blight
plans with free fat money
and wrecking balls
and writs of condemnation

waved like candy in front of drooling politicians
there was big money for demolition and construction
not painting or patching
there's no cashing in on that

there was no concern for time or memory
there was no conservative surgery
no thought about the complexity of cities
the ties of neighborhoods, or
the value of history

history was something in books
not in landscapes and buildings

there was only chaos and blight
old junk to be cleared
poor people
to be removed
a blank slate to be had
for highways
and modern mega structures
and everything new

the city was old, they worshiped new

the downtown was old...dilapidated
disposable to them

they said:
down with the old movie theaters
down with the old stores
down with the old downtown buildings
down with the old downtown

the ripped-out trolleys
were already old news
so now they ripped out
the grid streets too

sidewalks...who needs them?
pedestrians...what's that?

this is modern America...
the land of highways and parking

but the small proprietors grumbled
they wanted to stay put
not pay high rent
or spend their own tax money
to attract chain store competition

they liked things as they were
but their pleas went unheard
by the shadows waiting to cash in

their plan meant clearance
it was simple
minded you didn't think
too hard about loss or the future

clearance...then build a mall
it'll be a big hit
our detailed analysis says so

so like a child who swings arms in a fit
they knocked the blocks apart
and down came history
demolished
and if there were tears in the dust
no one saw them

they carted away the city's heritage in dump trucks
and dumped it in the dustbin of history

a hundred-plus buildings blasted
and in their place, a mall
plopped like a big dump
like a meteor from Mars
right in the middle of Main Street
blocking, clogging
and confusing everybody with
one-way patterns of disorientation

oh, they cut ribbons
and sang praises of progress
happy that something changed
but the new was not new for very long
and in no time the mall sat near empty

and now there it is...still sitting, crumbling
a boondoggle of tragic proportions
all alone in my desolate downtown
like an ancient monument
to perfidy and dumb greed

and the backdrop of vacant storefronts
the empty rooms in spared structures
the boarded windows
the broken dreams
the silence

nothing left but ghosts
faded memories
and nothing renewed at all

the heart and soul of the city
crushed by the dark myth of progress

and down there still, buried under concrete
are the ghosts of those who walked
talked shopped sold and celebrated life here
in this little mill town city

they lie waiting
like sleeping seeds
down in the dirt
dreaming of demolition
dreaming of old patterns
waiting for new eyes to see
waiting for new life to emerge
from the wreckage of hope
and the myth of progress reconceived.

clowns

the town on the edge of my city is a whore

it will take anything
anywhere
anyway it can get it
as long as it pays

the stains and scars
wide open on the landscape
bare no shame for the world to see

a smear of colored schlock
signs shouting the obscenity of familiar brands
bombarding our sanity
in a roadside blur of big boxes
big parking lots
and super-sized grease pits
to congeal your Styrofoam arteries

the sweat of Shanghai
packaged on an oversea odyssey
to meet the needs of your low-budget lifestyle
slave-labor certified
though warning! may contain lead

the highway they study
the cars they count
the conflicted propensity to crash
and assure your jacked insurance

the mystery sidewalks
buried in the blind minds of unsuited planners
or extracted without plan
and leading no one to nowhere

the abandonment for write off
the empty cinder-block boxes
like signposts of a quick profit shipped elsewhere

the historic fragments of embarrassment
eulogized on little plaques
like rusty reminders of a day-late culture

the empty benches barely
shaded by transplant junipers
browning in despair

the open scrape wounds
pouring silt without sieve
to choke streams with
the brown blood of the land
uncovered like buried spirits unseen

and everywhere
you see clowns

it's a shopping circus
with funny cars
and fat clowns
and hardly happy clowns
and dirty clowns
and little clone clowns
and clueless clowns
worrying and hurrying around

everywhere you look
you see clowns.

the world is your oyster

in America
we know no limits
so don't mess with our freedom of choice

in the land of something for nothing
we want it all:
fame, fortune, deliverance
a road to paradise paved with gold

and we want it on the cheap

the myth of manifest destiny
says take, so we do
and let nothing stand in our way

not beaver, not Indian, not buffalo
not distance or height or time

a vast world without bounds
to absorb our shit smog and sin

to drink up our pollution
our stormwater laden with filth
chock full to make dead fish glow in the dark

the smokestacks cough out
monoxides and mercury
dioxides to trap heat in the air...

wait, wait, wait!
hold on
is this another tree hugger plea?

look...don't give me that environmental gibberish
keep that granola crap to yourself

we like meat and hummers, baby

we drive wide rides
that drink gas like we drink Budweiser

and we own guns
and we'll use them!

we're made in America
in her likeness
big bad and bold
and this is our country

we're number one, motherfucker!
and the future is now, so
you're either with us or you're against us
and God help you if you're against us, cuz
we do whatever we please.

we have nothing to fear

they live in fear
these men at the top

and they use this fear
to generate more fear

to keep people scared
open to manipulation
and cowering to obey

but fear feeds on the soul
eats it
covers it like fungus
destroying hope
confidence
freedom

fear is the dry rot
in the foundation of civilization
the ultimate cancer
the ultimate winner

and you can almost see it
taking its victory lap
as people peek through drawn drapes
and support drawn guns
and support lying leaders
who tell us
we must not let the terrorists win
we must stay the course
forever vigilant
forever paranoid
forever scared

while we're bamboozled
with propaganda
notions of nationalism
and the sanctimonious charge of
our own religious fervor

we bow down like children
and give up our rights with a shrug

yet it is this fear
that covers everything with its stink
blinding us to the understanding
that because of our fear
the terrorists may have already won.

lost

her shoes don't match
except for the scuffs

the broken down baby carriage
broken off wheel
carries all of the broken down scraps
of her broken down life
but no baby

though she was a baby, once
maybe cradled swaddled
doted on cooing, but

now a wilted flower
with faded patterns
the torn dress
stained and stinking

she slumps down
broken down
broken heart
curbside
and flips through her pocket book
frenzied—

"oh my keys...oh my life...
have you seen them?"

with frazzled hollow eyes she cries:
"my keys...my life...
oh, I'm just about ready to kill myself!"

"I can't find my keys...can somebody help me?"

books

you are not going to get it
from television

sorry, but you won't find it there

don't think that sound bites
will teach you anything
other than confusion

you need the back-story unmentioned

the talk-show shills
grinding a point of view
sputtering hate
and fashioning scapegoats
will teach you nothing
except the wrong way to point your finger

our system of inculcation
teaches kids what to memorize
and spit out on tests
and how to sit still and swallow
prescribed perspectives
to mold the good worker
the good soldier
who won't question
and do what is told
while learning to comply with
the whitewashed version

you have to dig deeper
spend some time
the old-fashioned way
borrow or buy books
while you still can
then hunker down
and read them

if you really want to know
the truth is in there
hiding in the right places
waiting for you to connect the dots

it won't be easy
like flipping channels
but nothing that matters ever is.

sales

the sales girl gets her orders:
ten cases of Chardonnay
she has to meet her quota
or her paycheck just won't pay

she works on tight commission
gets a fraction of the take
brings in all the business
for the owners on the make

she's the lowest rung
to be stepped on
by all

with incessant demands
by grasping hands never satisfied
never enough
to fill the corporate mouth
with its daily blood

the logic of extraction
to drain every penny
to slam the lid on every deal
like the thunk of the treasure trunk closing

trained in shark logic
with brains that know only hunger
it is a ceaseless moving
toward the scent of the kill
the art of the deal
like the art of war

a battle of cut throats
behind smiles with unseen scars
brought home nightly
to throw at shouting walls
like drained wineglasses

and the sales girl
a sad little Lowman
lugging her bottle bag
gets used up like a peon
and spit out like a pit
to make room for the next one
waiting in line.

keeping the crimp on freedom

so here we are in the land of the free
locking up more people
than anybody anywhere—
more than any bad-guy dictatorship in the world

yet we wage war in the name of freedom
as liberators
the mailmen of democracy
delivering packed slogans
through the barrel of a gun

yes, our freedom is real
but our freedom is a slogan too
contradictions
navigated in cloaks of melanin
and sanctified payment plans

pharmaceuticals pushed and peddled
to a doped-up country
but don't try to self-medicate
no toot for you like Washington or Jefferson
and don't grow your own
no sacred smoke or parchment for
radical declarations or constitutions

to become fodder
for a system of perpetual imprisonment
where souls are sucked dry
in subsidized housing
for the dangerous classes—
a safety valve for the echoes of slavery
containers of discontent
and peon labor
where brutalized exiles
in cement boxes
are quarantined
then branded
and recycled without reform
like pawns in some sick strategy
of rural economic development:
jobs for the hinterlands to
placate politicians
while keeping certain people in their place
keeping power where it lies
keeping up the lies to justify crimes
that keep the crimp on freedom
over here in the land of the free.

running on empty

it must suck
that you can no longer afford to drive

with gas at...what? twenty dollars a gallon
who can?

only the gilded
not the formerly middle class

it must suck
that your American dream
has lost so much value
and your two SUVs
just sit there

you must have lost a bundle in equity

maybe you can telecommute?
but it must get boring as hell
and lonely too
way out there
in your mortgaged desolation

remember when isolation
was an aspiration
when cities were a stepping stone
to leave behind?

remember when sidewalks were forgotten
and density meant a slum
and rusting railroads were ripped up for highways?

now look at the misdirected disillusion
out there on the fringes
the disappointment
debt and depreciation
disengaged from the dream
detached from the world
disconnected from all that's solid
wallowing in a myth gone sour
wondering what went wrong
and wondering who to blame.

freedom of speech

they pulled the exhibit
and closed down the hall

too controversial for the new freedom

to challenge the president
in such a direct way

to challenge a nation
with its insecurity

to challenge free speech
by using it

to confront so directly
leaves them stuttering with rage

such effrontery
to face open dialogues
with a mouth
begging to be covered

seeking what is really open
by asking the wrong questions
by taking the seditious perspective
and challenging the norms of conformity
with words too free to speak

by questioning what we are really defending
when we claim to defend freedom.

the right to be left alone

seems the FBI has been breaking the rules
bypassing FISA, the secret court
in direct defiance of federal law

how do you like that for trust-us logic?

spying on thousands of Americans
with national security letters unauthorized

demanding the works
on anyone
with reasons unstated
they trample the Constitution
with jackboots of fear

Big Tele said okay
and gave them all the records
even those unasked for
in case they're ever needed

the phone records
the transcripts
the e-mails
the browsing

the director says he's sorry
it won't happen this way again
abuse of privacy, we admit
we broke the law back then

he asks for our forgiveness
asks people just to trust
says they are only protecting us
so we're not turned to dust

but should we trust the powers
and let them see through walls
and listen to the emanations
from our private calls?

let them read our records
and snoop by undetected
profile all the people
all for our own protection?

classify our habits
assign us scales of threat
determine what's "unreasonable"
with no real standard met?

and what if you might question them
and challenge their cold lies
and what if you're not comfortable
beneath their prying eyes?

will they call you traitor
and file you away
locked up without the recourse
of the courts to hear your say?

and maybe then
if this is you
you'll question what they say
question whether the fishbowl life
must be the American way.

Godness

we try to comprehend God
and we just can't do it

our brains are simply not designed
to grasp Omnipotence

yet we try

and we assume
and make religion out of it

and I wonder if God gets a kick out of creation
down here floundering?

all the people thinking it's in the books
not able to visualize in any other way
what we will never know
and can only feel
if we stop talking
and learn to listen with other ears.

the gift

the open notebook sits
like a beggar's hand
asking for a gift from heaven

the blank page
a pale face pleading
with torn fabric
and the black smears
of misdirected wanderings

some days it is an empty hand waiting
with a growl in the bowel of a starving soul

and some days it is overheard words
the prose of street talk
or the tragic headlines
that wrap shoeless feet

and there are hallowed days when
a gift is placed into waiting hands
like an unexpected valentine in a big red bow

little teardrop flames
revealing prerecorded messages

with words
like timeless tunes
talking
taking tours
touching
teardrops cried
for new tomorrows

celestial gumdrops
placed softly
as if from angels
sowing starlight seeds
that burst forth like bright rainbows

so you bow down
kiss the ground
let tears of gratitude flow
for the sustenance
and symbol
that there is something beyond
this hard pavement
and this blank page.

rock stars

we cut down Laurel Canyon
to Sunset Boulevard

the mansions of Bel Air line the road

the car in front's a Lamborghini
and the lights behind us, maybe a cop

a few miles down Sunset, we park
the meters don't apply at night

we walk to the famous club
dreaming ourselves the featured show

it's a parade of freaks, with big hair
and spandex, heels and leather
wannabe rock stars flood the scene
leaving leaflets that litter the sidewalk

"check that shit out!"
and there, across the street
walks a dude in black leather
long spiked-up hair
with chains that dangle
and a leash that drapes from his hand
to the neck of his girlfriend
who walks in front like a heavy metal pet

she has pink hair blown everywhere
big tits busting out of her lace underwear
her only clothes, except the spike heels

we laugh and get in line in front of the club

we know the door dude, so get waved ahead
grabbing two bunnies in line to take with us

lipstick, hairspray and heels
perfumed porn stars or neophytes trying

the amps so loud, we talk in clipped shouts
and somebody yells, who's buying?

we get our drinks, and head backstage
where the bunnies know one of the bands

the singer sits on the couch with two girls,
a straw in his hand and he's smiling

our bunny says, oh!...it's bitching to see you
runs over and lays her lips on him

in no time she's holding the straw in her hand
sliding it in her mouth pretending

everyone laughs, thinking decadent love
as she sucks up the nose candy waiting

then the band is ready to hit the stage
to rock to the sound of heavy metal
guitars and loud amps and big booming drums
and a bass that rattles the rafters

and here we are, in the land of rock dreams
forgotten hair bands and lace ladies
a party of joyful debauchery
on the Sunset Strip in the eighties.

fear and loathing

there was a time when
a new neighbor meant
a pie
a welcome basket
a housewarming party

but that was then...

the for-sale sign
hung on the house
for over a year

maybe people were spooked
by the "seized" sign
nailed to the front porch
proclaiming forfeit
for a drug deal on tape?

but now the sign is down
and the new neighbors are in
and if you walk by
you'll meet the growl sounds
of their big bad German Shepard

and there's a new sign in front
that doesn't say for sale
or welcome
or home sweet home
it says: warning! house protected by...

so no pies arrive
and if the house is warm
we'll never know
if it's sweet or soured by fear

I wanted to introduce myself
say welcome
tell them it's a good neighborhood

I wanted my kids to be able to knock and say
trick or treat
or can he come out and play
or would you like to buy a raffle ticket?

but instead
we just follow directions
and keep out.

hazardous to your health

they say that toys are contaminated
with lead, like old-paint houses
and many novel medicines
have the side effects of graveyards

they've found that certain cribs
are killing sleeping babies
and certain plastic baby bottles
leach out some harmful stuff

it's been noted by the scientists
that the food you eat is poison:
laced with hormones and pesticides
and trans fats to fill your arteries

and that water from the tap you drink
is awash in our pollution
and the air is greenhouse choked
in a smog-shroud ozone haze

they say the fish are loaded
with heavy-metal toxins
so if you are with child, please
watch how much you eat

they say that meat is coated
with bacteria like e-coli
dripping blood drop antibiotics
to alter your resistance

they think there are bad chemicals
in deodorant and toothpaste
and the Teflon flaked off in your eggs
just might cause you cancer

like every other substance
that you touch or taste or breath
the fruits of modern progress
to put you on your knees

and all that tastes so scrumptious
will elevate your pressure
and make you fat
or clog your heart
and rob you of life's treasures

and sex that once was ecstasy
now might give you AIDS
and even fruit and vegetables
are sprayed in toxic ways

but don't you worry 'bout anything
though everything is frightening
'cause worrying too
will weaken you
and also help to kill you.

cancel the subscription

keeping up with the world
will make you delirious

try reading a newspaper every day
and see what you see

what a way to start the morning:
coffee, toast
and tragedy

taking it real and bitter
engaged in the myth
that knowledge matters

keeping tabs on what condition
our condition is in:

yes, there's still a war or two

yes, the stock market's
still falling

yes, gas is stilling going up
and so is food
and so is inequality
and so is the temperature
and so is your blood pressure
and so are your taxes
and so is just about everything except
your quality of life

let's see who's cheating:
everybody

let's check on cities:
a cacophony of senseless murder and corruption
abandonment and poverty

let check on the world:
still heading toward catastrophe

or if you can't take all this reality
cancel the subscription
and check on the trivia instead
the other reality
that makes us feel better
distracts us from the facts
as we tune out
wallowing in dirty laundry
dumb deeds
famed fools
and televised humiliation

all to make us feel better
by covering our eyes
to what's really going on.

dreaming of crocus

woke up to a dark day
and had a premonition
to stay in bed
pull the covers
over my head
and stay down

there's ice out there
whipping winds
and white-out flurries

it's the dreary days of February
when the harsh winter winds blow cold
and the weight of the world
seems to bear down hard and heavy
like wet slush on your soul

the moon stares
ominous white
and the tensions of life's abrasions
rub raw, and get pulled a little tighter
when the planets align in such a way

I heard the voice say
don't move
don't go out
don't answer the phone
just lie low

so I rolled over
and pulled up the covers
ducking depressing emanations
from the dark-day Februaries
in the winter of my discontent

waiting for warmer days
when the waves are on the upswing
and the sun reaches out
as the earth tilts to it
shattering cold demons
and starting everything anew.

masochists

you see the sticker still stuck
clinging to a dirty beat-up pickup truck
proclaiming democratic triumph
nearly four years old

it is an open question
for connoisseurs of social consciousness:
is it shameless ignorance
or simply the vanity of victory?

content to be seen as winners
and blind to the tragic mess
that trails in the wake of their choice?

but I can see the rust that flakes
in the wake of their poverty
contradicting their support
with their private pain

the grimy jeans and stained shirts
a whiff of deprivation
clinging to soiled caps
and missing teeth to bark broken words
about guns and unborn children
about liberals and fags
niggers and wetbacks

the clear enemy and opposition of their lever pulls

imagine their grasping confusion
as they carry the welfare cheese
over the thresholds of their broken trailers

as they share cheap beer with the neighbor
who lost two sons over there
defending their servitude

wondering how things have gotten so wrong:
all these bad times
and others to blame

if they could only get rid of the traitors and heathens
everything would right itself

life would become pro again
(through righteous wars)

prosperity would trickle down again
(through the benevolence of pickpockets)

and good old American values
would again reign supreme
so that shotguns
can forever hang proud
above bold bumper stickers
naming winners

proclaiming the victory of their team
the names they know only in name
and the politics they know only in myth
as they strangle their own necks
with choices abstract from their suffering.

the invisible hand

the theory is
markets
unfettered
untethered to place
unrestricted by laws
and regulations
work best

gloves-off competition:
the ideal

monopoly: the undisputed champ

but lo, a paradox:
here we have a sport
where to be undisputed
is to summons sanctions—
to get knocked down a few pegs
or disassembled into smaller pieces

is this big government
showing big business who's boss
confronting the behemoths
for the little guy?

or if you look behind the curtain
do you see an occasional circus show
to give cover to the real deal?

where laws are written
by those who profess hatred of laws

where rules are created
to protect the rule haters

where government
is the hand maiden
and backdoor lover
of those who profess hatred
of government's meddling hands

subsidies for every deal—
taxpayers on the hook
underwriting private profit
in a game called economic development

or benevolent government with a bailout
for those too big to fail

the bigger the business
the more visible our open hands

mom and pops go begging
while multinationals bag the big bucks

CEOs with treasure severances
sucker workers
with pink-slip retirements

the three-job family
pays the full freight
while yacht man
off-shores the write-off

social welfare is demonized dependency
while corporate welfare
is the normalized golden goose
to worship at the altar of entitlement

the market, not free
held by two invisible hands
one, covering two faces
and the other, pulling boot straps
from Brooks Brothers.

one and all

here we have
with each new day
the dawn and slow death
of the human spirit

waking to sunshine or clouds
confronting first thoughts
while shedding dreams or nightmares

the gradual recognition
the tension of pending duties

and with every new day
there are choices:
engagement or ignorance
confrontation or flight
narcissism or brotherhood

but our system suffers

we are home alone
in ignorant bliss
tuned out on trivia
and ignoring the tragedy
as our democracy withers on the vine

but the world goes on
ignored or not

yet each of us
alone in our isolation
are part of this daily tide
like water molecules
that make up an ocean

to pretend otherwise
is to evaporate
powerless
manipulated
and channeled

but if oceans contain all
then only together
can we turn the tide
like an ocean
breaking barriers
jumping borders
and smoothing out the rough shores
of our battered republic

not alone
like isolated grains
only together is there power
to confront
like an ocean.

skin

look at the girls these days
showing all that skin:
bellies, boobs, butts

what's up with that?

they can't all be hookers

you see cleavage
busting out of tight tops
the curve contours of
the surgeon's knife

you see bellybuttons
poked with rings
and in back
winged tattoos
fly above the whale tails
flapping up the crack
peeking up from the bowels
and out the back

everywhere you look
it's skin and underwear
coming up for air
saying to everybody, look at me!

there is no shame in porn-star fashion:
even the fat folds of the muffin top
flap in the wind exposed

and you have to wonder
is that intended?

all these girls, from
patched up old ladies
to kids too young to touch
all with the same message:
wanna fuck?

I bet most of them
don't put out like pigs

they're just playing the part
following the pack
programmed with the imagery of
their world's warped reality

and I bet some day
they'll have to explain
when old images surface
with a question:
"Mommy, is that you?"

1040

it's the last minute
to compile the ledgers
the doleful accounting
of wages and obligations

the coerced contribution
toward my government:
the take of my toil
they use to pave roads
to build schools
to pay off friends
and fund wars in my name

it is blood money
and tribute
the tithe offering
to the god of commerce
and subterfuge

a duty avoided
only by prison

it is not a giving
but a taking back
of overcharges

my grudging tribute
already spent
two generations out
the borrowed interest
on my grandchildren's future

but if I deduct
for the folly of these fools
for all the misspent waste
the corruption
and the sanctified crimes
justified in my name
I'd ask for it all back
principal and interest
to withhold
in peaceful protest
until the day arrives
when the meanings are restored
when words are no longer convoluted slogans
when justice is real
when peace means peace
when the people are heard
and when waste is something they do
with their own money
not mine, through the puppets in their plays.

the home of the governor

it's the capital city

the neighborhood is the South End

the bottom

what a collection it has:
historic shells
vacant history clad in a veneer of chipped paint
crumbling bricks
and plywood

the governor's mansion sits on the edge

he looks out drawn drapes
through windows without plywood shutters
and what does he see?

happy people holding hands
walking
talking
going shopping?

or does he see a picture he can't tell
with dirt and grime and gunshot hell:
derelict dry rot
hopeless homelessness
blood dripping drug scenes?

to help, does the state have a plan?

does he know the city has a plan?

does the city know it has a plan?
can anyone find it
sleeping in the dust on the shelf?

I've been told it is a plan of hope
and change
and new days coming
the sun shining bright

it is a plan with music
that sounds like saws
hammers
nails being sunk
into new shingles
to stop the music of the rain
from hitting the floors
and making the walls buckle
and groan and crumple

it is the sound of kids laughing
people talking
workers in the morning
leaving with a kiss
the door lightly closed
toward the dawn of a new payday

but what music does the governor hear?

is it the sound of silence
or sound bites
or the drapes drawn shut?

the suburbanites

they bought their house
out on the far-flung fringe
at the end of a new cul-de-sac subdivision
gated and guarded by watchman

they don't want anyone they don't know
cutting through or passing by

no riffraff

and no mixing with other types

they like isolation
and similarity
it gives them comfort
peace of mind
like their neighbors
white and making out all right

they feel camaraderie in shared seclusion

and though they have no choice
they'd prefer to drive anyway
though the cost is now killing them

they've seen on TV that
it's getting real bad out there these days
and it makes them nervous

they want security

and as far as all that planning baloney
about sidewalks
connections
public space
and density?

no, they want to be buffered

and they don't want anything to change
they want everything
(except resale value)
to stay just as it is

pull up the drawbridge
to keep out the invading hordes

that's why you see those gates
and that guard:
to delineate
to differentiate
and to protect them
from all that rotten humanity.

here

here in the day
in 2008
we wait for our salvation

we wait for clarity
to clear the clouds
a rainstorm
to wash away troubles

we wait for the henchmen
to go back home
and give us back our country

we wait for the people
to wake to the world
and see it now more clearly

here in the day
I live my life
with tempered expectations
and warmer types of solitude
in peaceful contemplation

waiting for opposing views
to trade places for a day
to better see each other
and be open to other ways

I search for ways of evo-
revolution every day
for paths to take us past the past
and put us on the Way

here in the day
in 2008
we hold our breath and wait
and think about our children
and the future they might face.

money in the rainbow stream

there was a time when you could tell
the color of the dye that day
by the color of the nearby stream

and there was a time when
the river was so sullied
if you jumped in, you'd get sick

you could see little brown boats
with paper sails trailing
fighting maritime battles
against the red rag armada
or the paper cup navy in waiting

and there was a time when
the smokestack soot
blackened skies
like a thunderstorm pending
spewing indelible stains
and a symphony of coughs

yet these were the days when
the factories were full
and the hard-working man made a living

and these were the days when
the bars overflowed
and downtown was a big destination

the streets were a bustle
the trolley car clanged
and foreign tongues sung out new hope

the sounds of a mill town
the rumble of the freight train
the whistle of the work day ending

but now the crystal stream drinks dye no more
and the river runs blue like the sky

and there is no more soot
with the smokestacks asleep
above factories with bolts on the doors

the days of memory and nature are upon us
as frisky vines make love to plywood windows
and old bricks drop down like red hailstones
and trees spring through rotted roofs
to make starlight views of heaven

and I watch in sad awe
as the city crumbles back to its origins

thinking about green:
the green dye in the stream
the green pocketed to pollute
the green pocketed to close down
and the green now growing over everything.

take me to the river

there is a church
where I was a baby baptized
and a boy receiving first communion

inside is a dark booth
where I gave coerced confessions
passing nervous guilt through a metal screen

and up on the altar
like a good soldier
I've bowed my head
and clasped my hands
to receive the body and blood

the desecrated effigy
hangs up high
a reminder of his sacrifice

in memory of love eternal

and down below it
have passed
the blessed bodies
of my ancestors

but I am an exile apostate
of delusion
and certainty

open to understanding
other idols

believing all
and nothing

consecrated too
like a walnut in a drum
with bird blood ancient songs
and deep rhythms to convey

so now my church is the earth
and my god is closer
and farther
than ever

and that first church
forever sacred
won't see my shadow
until they roll me in
undaunted by lemmings
who cower in sin

and if I remember
to make out a will
my body will not be delivered

instead they'll scatter my ashes
down into the Mohawk River.

words

for every word
at least two meanings

and ways to speak
that say nothing at all

to say one thing
but intend its opposite

to jerk certain strings
in your heart

to use packaged slogans
and they do it all the time
to confuse
and rally your hate

to tell in plain language
or put it in a poem
with metaphor and simile to hide it

or leave it wide open
for others to adorn
and twist to suit to their purpose

to make characters and
put words in their mouths
and take an omnipotent view

like the Word
literalized God in a book
by divine pen
making worlds
and helping destroy them

the mind in words, ideas
as spirit manifest
mythical stories and songs
the human essence in language
yet nothing but words.

somewhere in the middle

it's possible
to love someone deeply
and to dislike them too
maybe even deeply

it's possible to hold someone
so tightly
that you push them away

it's possible
to make such perfect plans
that everything goes awry

it's possible
to care so much
about something or someone
that you stop caring

is it possible
that every human emotion
needs its opposite to exist?
that you can't have one
without the other
like day needs night
positive and negative
embedded in
the circuitry of existence?

I suspect the trick
if there is one
is to find some balance
some in-between
where the pendulum of our polarity
is in equilibrium
if only
temporarily.

mutants

skinny, wrinkled, bespectacled
with a long white coat, and

in his hand, the glass flask glistens
as he lifts it for their inspection, and says

this tap water
is just like the water
millions of people drink every day

in it, a vast array
ignored by regulators
these untested waters
pure to the eye, untreated
and deemed safe by the rules
are a glistening cloak
choked with a cornucopia
of pharmacological effluvia

the list includes:
nicotine
antibiotics
anticonvulsants
mood stabilizers
sex hormones
and a slewy soup
of over-the-counter
drain-dumped junk

he says, people take pills
people secrete
and people flush toilets

he says, we don't test
so we don't know
the cumulative impact of exposure

but our initial analysis
shows alarming effects
shows we might want to
watch what we flush
and start treating what we dump

so the reporters take dutiful notes
and publish hardly-read stories
while the public drinks up
unaware of the three-legged frogs
leaping through the coal mines of progress

and they never question
the scrambled-egg organs
the mutant features
like milkless mammaries
and shrinking testicles
or the shrinking brains
shrinking in blind unawareness
shrinking and never noticing.

vice

there are timeless desires
glorified
and intensified
by our system of hypocrisy

to make victimless a crime
to promote, then scold
or imprison to control

seductive sex
in all the imagery
enticing perpetual youth
eternal beauty
and easy love

yet don't sell your body
in the marketplace of everything
or make love outside the fashion

don't grow your own
though just say yes
and eat their tainted chemicals

there is a pill for everything
and laws to keep the prisons filled

don't pay the bookie
but play the lottery

worship capitalism
yet criminalize
its informal application

freedom is virtue
freedom is vice

sex is beauty
sex is vice

sanctified gambling
gambling is vice

sex and money and something for nothing:
the foundation of the republic
the foundation of vice
an excuse
to make freedom a slogan.

little Mimi

she's about four-foot nothing
give or take a few inches for the heels

and she's got the works:
the hairdo
the nails
the make-up
the get up

there she goes
walking that high-heel tip-toe totter
trying not to twist an ankle
as she lugs her bags across the parking lot

but she should be wearing climbing boots
because she's got a small mountain to deal with:

just look at her rig!
it's the Titanic on wheels
about ten feet high
and I'm dying to see how she gets in it
let alone drives it

she opens the back door
slings in the bags
over the shoulder
in one smooth motion like a pro

then she opens the front door
barely reaching the handle
takes off her heels
throws them inside
backs up a bit
to get a running start
and with two bounding steps
she grabs the doorjamb
and vaults herself in

back it goes
almost hits the next row of cars
then she turns the corner
and up it goes
back wheel over the curb, bah-boom
and she's off:

big blown blond hair
big white shades
and gleaming red nails
stick up over the steering wheel
of this beast of a gas guzzler
as she roars off to some soulless suburbia somewhere
with a license plate that says:
me me me.

second hand

the young child wants young daddy's lap
so daddy eats by reaching around
while the boy clings, head against chest

the young mother looks on
letting daddy console
doesn't want to mess up
her perfect outfit
perfect hair
and manikin makeup

their eyes watch the boy
then dart round the restaurant
in self-conscious, novice glances

as if to say, wow
seems only last year
we were young and fancy free
but look at us now
with responsible days
to care for our new bundle of joy

they finish eating
and get up to leave
with the boy still clinging
and mommy applying fresh lipstick

then out the door, her cigarette's lit
puffing smoke rings up through the air

and into the car
daddy at the wheel
while sonny sits and breaths
and mommy checks herself in the mirror
puffs and drags
sucks and exhales
while I watch and wonder
from my table by the window
as the air in their car grows dark.

cracked

the description said "new"
but the book arrived not new

it was dirty, worn
and had a cracked binding

at least it wasn't underlined

WARNING: all used book dealers are not alike

I e-mailed my complaint and got a quick response:
"when we mailed it, it was new"

motherfuckers

naturally, I ripped off a rating to post on Amazon...
but then I got thinking...from the Bronx...just a few
hours away...
has my address...only has four ratings
so this slam pulls business down hard...

so after a few days, I deleted it
no sense having my tires slashed, or worse
over a ten-dollar book of Bukowski poems

but that cracked binding
how it bugged me

I didn't mind the dirt or frayed edges so much...
but I fucking hate cracked bindings!

so though usually gentle,
I started to abuse the bitch—
tore the cover
dripped coffee on it
spilled red wine, which soaked through
like a blood-stain wound

I bent it backwards in five places
making six cracks altogether...snap...crackle...pop...
and I even ripped out a few poems I didn't like...
crumbled up and flung like Hank should have done

and finally, I took out a big blade
and jammed it right through...
impaled like a shish kabob

and there it sits, atop the bookshelf
a stabbed, cracked and tattered sculpture

though it makes me wonder
if there's something wrong
with me...
if I'm not the one with the cracked binding.

holes and poles

here we have the hole
and the pole
always seeking
searching for each other

hardwired from birth
the forbidden fruit
the apple of everyone's eye
be fruitful and multiply
to nurture nature's message

it seems so simple, animal-like
the lowest bugs can do it
but mix in media, money
and man
confusion sets in

take a day in the news
to seek some examples:

a new survey says
teen girls
do it when they please
and one fourth of their holes
are dripping with disease

so telling these kids
to just close their legs
no way that's gonna work
instead we should tell them
to wrap that pole
or stay home and give it a jerk

then we have the gym teacher
with urges he can't reason
but coach, she's underage, you fool
now you'll be tried for treason

and a rapist let out of prison
went looking for a piece
and they got it all on cameras
trying to force-feed his relief

and the bishop preaches morality
and he knows just what to say
been busy protecting choir boys
from horny priests too gay

and then we have
the TV star
who says she used to dance
and slide her hole
against a pole
so drooling fools would glance

and hoot and howl
and make her play
they'd stay around all day
but she didn't mind their company
'cause her pussy made them pay

and finally we have the bombshell
at the capital of New York
it seems the governor's poked his pole
in expensive hooker hole

paying cash
to get his kicks
and do his nasty things
but they caught the crime
on wiretap
a tax-evasion sting

so the crusader who fought corruption
and squawked about reform
went down another hypocrite
where shame is now the norm

went down on a golden carpet
where only emperors play
to poke their gilded poles in holes
for which they have to pay

and maybe when
they pull it out
and put their poles away
they'll bring some STD back home
for wifey when they lay

and so with sex
we're all confused
and know not what to choose
a faithful love
or virtual fucks
or simple one-night screws.

the treadmill

what version are you on?

do you have the latest release
the latest upgrade
the latest model?

or are you an error message
in the game of perpetual obsolescence?

maybe a secret rebel fighting next week's iteration
with a version working just fine
feeling sympathetic toward choked landfills
gagging on growth
seeing limits beyond the comprehension of capitalism
which calls into question
the cult of continuous consumption?

always more
everything new
all that's solid
melting according to plan

the progress of profit.

HMO

don't get sick
in America, it could
send you straight to
the poor house

and since we got rid of
all the poor houses, you
may find yourself out
on the street

oh, so you have insurance, huh?
a lucky one covered, just
a deductible, that's all

this belief
born of inexperience, never
having experienced denial of coverage, never
having confronted
a health money organization, never
having challenged
the bureaucratic juggernaut

insuring profit
insuring the bottom line
insuring they will find
every conceivable loophole
to deny

so you paid, you say
every premium
never late?

so?
read your contract

but how can you deny? my
husband is dying! will
die without treatment!

how can I pay cash?
I can't afford to pay $60,000
to reattach these two fingers!

I guess I'll take the index for $20,000
and eat noodles
here in the new economy of sorrow

where progressive government
is reviled
and big business
is exalted

a system of rigged influence
insuring not you, but
profit over people remains

so sorry
about your loved one
who might have been saved

so sorry
about the bankruptcy
the lost house, job
or your sick spouse preexisting

so sorry
you aren't Canadian, French, English, Scandinavian
living in lands with government's meddling hands

you are an American
in the land of compassionate conservatism
where it is corporate America
who stands by your sick bed
offering you an invisible hand.

shell shocked

in the morning
when I sit reading or writing
I can hear the footsteps:
clunk...clunk....clunk
slowly
the old man with his plastic bag
his dirty blue coat
dirty blue cap
and wrap-around cataract shades
tromps down the driveway
of the apartment building next door

he waits for the VFW van
or a taxi to take him wherever he goes

last year he had a Pontiac
which he would sit in for hours
smoking cigarette after cigarette
with the engine running

sometimes when other cars pulled in
he'd just sit there
blank stare
blocking the way
puffing away
looking through his dark shades to nowhere

I would see him whip into traffic
without looking or slowing
and a few times I heard the screech
but never a crash

or maybe he did crash somewhere
because now he just stands there
in the same place as before
right in the middle of the driveway
puffing and thinking his thoughts
without his car

I tried saying hello a few times
but he just stared
blank straight ahead
and for all I know
that's how he's been
ever since he returned
from that big bad second world war.

weapons of mass confusion

they said
there were weapons of mass destruction
but the only place they found them was
inside their heads

yet this was proof enough for them...
they had their secret justifications
that only the insiders knew

and there was the pretext
made up
to cover their tracks:
the door opened
by three thousand dead bodies
thanks to mad Moslems
from some far away place

fear became the new pastime
an Archimedean lever
to manipulate the masses

they used the media to help them
to stir up confusion and hate

so the left hand faked
and the right hand
moved the shell over a few countries
where there was oil
and old vendettas

they said it would stop terrorism
but it only made matters worse

so now the bombs
ring out a song of freedom
with hollow words
that hide what is true

while the real enemies elude us:
our old allies hiding in caves

and there should be no doubt
they're better off out of sight
as a perpetual excuse
to strip us of rights

and to keep the military cash register ringing
playing their song called: the shock doctrine

and the melody is
the sound of blown-up infrastructure
making a harmony
with private contractors rebuilding it

and the orchestra is an army of mercenaries

and the conductor wears no clothes

and the audience is divided
into three sections:

up front, those sent to kill and die

behind them, the flag wavers

and up in the balcony, the ones they call traitors...
the ones with tears in their eyes.

don't let the door hitcha

goodbye Mr. President, goodbye!
glad to see you go

these past eight years
(jesus, has it been that long?)
have been such a sad sad time
thanks to you

under the reign of YOU
and your cronies
we've watched America
(and the world)
drop down...way down

not because of what someone did to us
but because of what we did to ourselves
thanks to you
and your supporters

from surplus to deficit
from peace to war
from prosperity to recession
from hope to fear

thanks for shit, Mr. President
sorry we didn't impeach your ass

if there's a God, I thank Him now
for finally setting us free
though the pain of your malfeasance
will live long after you're gone

you have fucked things up, so much
that the next generation
will suffer your legacy

and maybe this pain
will only lay the groundwork
for another cornpone Nazi
worse than you or your vice
who'll lead us right into your Armageddon

but until that day of rapture
I count each day a blessing
no longer under your tragic command

it is a sad, muted pleasure
to say so long bush league
relieved to say: see ya
but wondering why
the world had to suffer so much
and so long because of you
the monkey from Texas
who will be forever remembered as
the worst ever...
dumb and dangerous
feared and hated like Stalin
like Hitler
like Satan.

vigilantes

they hide out in the desert
with loaded rifles ready
hoping to take down their prey

they gather likeminded
to collar the scapegoats
and channel frustrations with hate

they practice with video games
shooting down the brown peril
sharpening skills
to keep out the hoards

backed by officials
who pander to insecurity
and make excuses
for the tax bill that's soared

they've forgotten their roots
where their ancestors came from
their grandparents
in the same desperate shoes

who came to America
the land of opportunity
huddled masses
who dreamed life anew

but the doors have slammed shut
to foreign tongue seekers
in these days of decline
and stoked fears

while we build our fences
that leak with bribed holes
and we terrorize the ones that are here

keeping them desperate
while they landscape our yards
and pick fruit for our tables for pennies

but when they seek justice
or lines to legitimacy
they find that
there just isn't any.

the ad busters

it was noted
in some scientific study
that strobe lights
can trigger epileptic seizures

this was the first thought
that entered Dr. Adman's head
when he heard the news

all across cyber space
wherever there was a computer terminal
there were people flapping about the floor
chairs kicked out
foaming, frothing in furious tremors

phones rang
and no one answered

people knocked on office doors
but no one came

and when they opened these doors and looked in
it was the same scene everywhere:
some unsuspecting soul
had turned on their computer
checked e-mail
checked the news
and there it was:
the flashing ad

some state-of-the-art technique
for maximum distraction
guaranteed to pierce your concentration
and tug your eyes away
toward the flickering pitch

a pulse so powerful
so insidious that
if you refused to look
refused to break your focus
and turn your attention
the throbbing ad
would enter a secret section of your brain
and send you flopping on the floor in a seizure:
punishment
for refusing to look
for trying to be
an ad buster.

reduction ad absurdum

the problems that governments confront
are rarely problems of simple math:
it's not usually: A+B=
it's more like: if A, then X; if B, then Z
so let's see, is it X or Z we need to please?

though simple math is often used
to confuse a process for a solution:
form a taskforce
do a study
quantify a portion of what's already known
and pass it off as accomplishment
like spending time
figuring out the likely winner
of a horse race
that's already run.

call waiting

I see it all the time now
people separating themselves
with their cell phones
inverting the myth of connectedness

here's the teen daughter
sitting at a restaurant with dad
not talking
not looking at him munching
enraptured in her trivia
holding her cell like the Rosetta stone

and here's the family man
sitting with wife and kids
body language says he's half out the door
at an angle
back to wife
and one leg off the bench in the aisle

all through dinner, clicking and staring
not looking at his family
saying nothing to the kids or wan wife
not really eating either

cell phone man
with his sport coat
and stupid shoes
wears a wedding ring
but not for long

as he clicks
and they click
and chat
about this crap
and that

out loud in the supper market
the subway
the bank

in meetings
in bars
at ballgames
and probably in church

looks freaky, doesn't it?
people talking to themselves
walking down the street with earphones
can't tell who's nuts or not

and it makes me nuts...
makes me want to bark out
"hey man!...anybody want to hear half my business?"

and in the car they say fuck the law
a gab away like crazy
connected in metal cocoons

everyone everywhere
connected yet disconnected
multitasking and missing out
one ear and one eye
in a river of humdrum cyber babble.

resale value

the central challenge
of urban planning is:
how do you get
a whole series
of separate real estate deals
to add up
to a real sense of place?

not a subdivision does a community make

not a scattering of isolated cul-de-sacs
everywhere farmland's for sale

not acres of paving for parking
where a car key is a necessity

not now when oil is a diminishing return
at a time of choked air by the carbon we burn
at a time when the climate is heating high seas
at a time when our budgets are tapped out and empty

and oh what a bundle
we've wasted so stupid
with patterns of infrastructure
that don't have a future

fleeing the city to hide from our fears
the sprawl and the gates where no place appears

just isolated houses, no diversity near
and the pleas of the planners for no one to hear

and big box shopping with credit cards maxed
and pissed off constituents who're all overtaxed
and can't sell their deals
like cars without wheels
'cause the gas to get there's too high.

stream with two names

over the rocks of ages
pours the blood of life

from mountaintop origins
pulled by gravity's rainbow

carving and scouring

diverted to quench thirsty throats
and dry lawns

hiding underground
in sinkholes and caves

running down 'round
to gather in pools
the spawn homes
of rainbows and browns
and the eels from the sea
that climb rock steps
to catch sight
of the eagles in flight

it flows past the land
worked in toil and sweat
where corn grows
and cows chew the hay

it weaves through little hamlets
from the days
when the farm and the market were one

through forests, then channeled
past factories, dumping
past smokestacks
that drift toxic winds

and down through the switching yards
where the clear blue
turns brown and air thin

the stream with two names:
Onesquethaw-Coeymans
gathers all of our hopes and fears:
clear sustenance, the bounty of life
and the trash from the industry of man

and the farmer stands
with his back to the wind

and his cows stand
with their hooves in the creek

and the trucker drives
with his load full of stones
blowing lime dust up through the air

and from the shore shoots a string
attached to a pole
attached to a hook

and up from the riffle
the snout of a trout
the splash of the tail
reflecting sunshine
and the face of the fisherman's smile.

it's getting hot out there

the mist shimmers
with the weight of eons' heat

accelerated by the hand of man
the loop feeds back
baking the earth
and drenching it
in angry whirlpools

the neighborhoods near the river
sit soaked in bloated water
and basements fill
to become new indoor pools

and the tree roots, like hydra hair
coming up for air
hundred-year-old monuments
battered down to the ground
crying maple teardrops

the power lines
just dangle there
not a pole upright
so sorry kids
it's lights out early
and no TV tonight

as the stink of spoiled food
wafts moldy on hungry tables
and the candlelight flickers
against dark faces that wait
and ask why?

is it nature or nurture
making sad survivors cry?

message to a young radical

the anarchy T-shirt snarls, his
matted ropes flap in the air
as he raises a fist in anger
and launches a rock through the window

in a blink he's down, fetal
on his back, truncheon whacks, then
zap-stung with a stun gun

this is no way to run a democracy!
what are you trying to teach people...
how to throw rocks?

this is the reasoning of mad generals
the fury of fists and gunpowder
not artistic logic, persuasion
by heartfelt reasoning
and higher symbolic gestures

you will never, rebel
never have enough might
to match their fight

and though you know you "know"
know you're right
feel it in your bones
feel nature like God
you must find a better way
to show the righteousness of your vision
if you seek allies and transitions

because rocks
bombs
and monkey wrenches
don't have enough love
to win out in the end.

getting by

the wrinkled man
all hunched and dirty
is always out there rummaging

his cart squeaks by on rusty wheels
resting as he fiddles plastic bags
dreaming of nickels

he gets pricked by things
an occupational hazard
of sharp shards
and the constant fear of needles

he comes home to his lonely room
with sticky hands and sore feet
up all night conversing with
dirty glass, tin cans, and plastic

he redeems the booty
for a paycheck
minimum wage
in multiples of five

just enough
to make the rent
buy cigarettes
and instant noodles

and if the gods are good that week
spare change for beer and cat food.

alone

their eyes don't look, but
they know you are there:
it is a steely side-vision disregard

their mouths don't smile, but
you know they could:
it is a withholding of better emotions

their hands to you motion not
no wave or finger beckons
only two that grip
and pursed lips to blow smoke

their high heels
and long legs
short skirts
and tight sweaters
seem to summon
but that message is for them
not you

their red lips contain stiff sentences
but you will never learn their illogic

you can only imagine their lipstick syntax

the romantic hears:
love songs, wild pleas, and sultry moans

the worn-souled cynic hears:
the screech of a wildcat
and broken glass

yet their curves contain multitudes
for the imagination

and that is the only way
that you will know them
so use it well.

feedback

they come by the carloads
to feel the power
of shared communion

it's a suburban Sunday
and a rock concert for God

the poser priest
blown big on the screen
with his magic-smoke-lightshow
to woo them

singing praise in His name
with high-voltage sacraments
and the wail of a big Marshall stack

hallelujah! they chant
with arms akimbo
asking God
for down payments
on the dream

if You will please grant me this
if You will please grant me that

I'll be better, I promise, I will...

they invoke the power
to rain down riches
convinced they are chosen
so special, looked after

and with the crowd
like a battle cry
they feel the power of group grasping
flowing like electricity through their souls

looking to fill empty meaning
empty minds, empty pockets
in a spectacle of modern deliverance

while the bearded priest
with his mail-order ordainment
blinds them with their longing
as he passes the basket
the yells, give...give!
and he receives.

smell the roses

the survey said
one quarter of all Americans
have switched religions
or shunned them altogether

they're searching for God
and don't know where to look

they've looked in the Bible
but only found contradictions:
the first part says, take an eye
and the second says, give it back

the book of the Jews, the Torah
was written for chosen people
but they're not Jews
so they're not sure
if they are chosen too

they've heard the rumors
of Islam's book
the one they call Koran
but Moslem jihad
or feminine repression
is not the life they plan

they've looked into
the lidded eyes
of Buddha with big belly

but they could not
see the Way
to nothingness
nor nirvana

none the less
they search and search
looking for salvation
trying to find
the prophet path
to absolve them
of their suffering

but there are others
and they see life
through eyes
shorn of religion

they're dazzled by
nature's bloom
and see the earth
as magic

and know that death
is part of life
both beautiful
and tragic

they feel the sun
against their face
and wondrous skies
fantastic

they listen to the songs of birds
and hear the voice of angels

baptized by the ocean breeze
and rainfall on their faces

the fertile plain
the mountain top
the grandeur of these places

they sing and dance
and love to laugh
and even sometimes cry

and they see God
inside their kids
by looking in their eyes

and here they find
all they need
true love enough
to live by.

daughter

the angel dances
draped in pink and gold
sings little bird songs

she paints pictures
and says
"I'm an artist, right Daddy?"

made speechless by her charms
I smile deeply
yet can't help but wonder:
what price the pain eventually?

who could I ever deem worthy to take her?

and how to protect her
from the future demons
she'll confront
in this enchanted forest world?

I hope there's an angel out there
to watch over my little angel.

going out

she puts on fishnet stockings
knee-high high-heeled boots
and lipstick to make a cherry blush

the blow-dryer whines in ecstasy
then lies hot to cool
while high cheeks turn rouge red
and bedroom eyes get lined in the mirror

the halter top not halting
yet gripping the suck-you-lance
of big paid-for boobs
bobbing above a bellybutton band of exposure

she whisks by in a cloud of perfume
blows a kiss and says
I'm going out...don't wait up...
just meeting a few friends...

so he walks in slow steps to the fridge
cracks a beer
and sits in the dark
sipping
and thinking
and wondering about trust.

freedom of choice

we nurture the virtue of choice:
freedom to pursue democratic vistas

yet the more important the choices
the more the choices diminish

you get to pick between
tweedle dumb or tweedle dee
this is your freedom

they are the slightest shade different
clearly in the middle

but what if your inclinations position you
closer to the edge?
what if the lemming path
is not of your liking...then what?

when freedom to choose means
either Sweet-and-Low or Equal

when substance has been bleached away
or considered too extreme

then there is no choice
but to choose
not to choose.

check please

do you want guns
or butter?
but don't say both

there's only so much
to go around

do you want to drop bombs
or do you favor social security?

it is a choice
in simple math
with big numbers:

what comes in is your taxes
the government's money

if you want to
waste it on war
guess what goes up?
or if not, then we must cut
but where? and what?

must we cut your retirement?
your street paving?
education
or healthcare?

or maybe you say:
to hell with school taxes
my kids are all grown?

or to hell with the highway budget
I can't afford to drive anyway...
so let the bridges fall?

or maybe you don't
believe in retirement
since the future is fucked
and we're all gonna die anyway?

but somebody, dear citizens
is going to pay the price
for empire
for backing the leaders of empire

the price for being serfs in this empire
with nothing to leave our children
except a machine gun
a prayer book
and a big bill.

the writer

the writer doesn't care
about contracts
or editors
or publishers

the writer doesn't care
about sales counts
or merchandizing
or image

the writer could care less
what the reviewers say
or what the judges think

and the writer doesn't give a shit
whether the work fits
with their preconceptions
or categories

yes, the writer wants to be read...
the writer does want readers

but really, readers or not...
writers just write

because they have to.

democracy of delusion

there are days when
the torment and trouble
of the world
seems so bad
so hopeless
so out of control
that you want to
take the newspaper
and fling it to the sky
like the tragic confetti of our reality

how much grief
how much stupidity
how many broken promises can we endure?

can any mind take it
and still remain whole?

so if you're one who pays attention
you better learn to laugh...
develop a sick sense of humor, like a shell
which can embrace the day saying, okay...
let's see what horrors await our inquiring eyes today...
oh look, the stock market's crashed...
oh boy, a new war's been started

and look at our cities in shambles...the gun shots...
corrupt cops...senseless murder...blood in the streets...
debauchery in high places

this is better than fiction:
a woman's flung her kids from a bridge...
and here's a good one
a father's microwaved his infant daughter...
and there's an evangelist preaching against vice
who pops meth and takes it in the ass at night...
and a school teacher who likes little pricks...
and here we go, another politician caught
with his pants down and his hand in the cookie jar...

the country's going bankrupt
and heading for depression
and mainstream looks like tabloids
saying the world is going to end

and it goes on and on
endlessly
every day
like blood spurting through a bullet hole
dripping black words of despair without hope

a rolling tickertape of tragedy
ceaselessly assaulting our sensibilities

so I can almost understand
these people who have tuned out

who can't bear the burden

they don't read about
or think about
all this reality

it's just too much to take

so they've decided to stop looking
and get lost in trivia instead
virtual realities, and other
altered states of ignorant bliss

but then I say no...sorry folks
you are not absolved from awareness
if turning your back means being misled

the puppets and fixers can't act alone, unsanctioned
they need your vote of implied approval
a majority to represent

and if you can't see the clothes of your emperor
if you can't tell a slogan from a lie
if you can't recognize a diversion from an issue

if your ignorance allows
the election
of murders and thieves
who ransack in our name
all because you haven't taken the time
to know beyond sound bites
or don't even bother
to go in the booth

then the problem
my friend
is you

because you
tuned out
and let them.

perfect values

the man with the smiling face promises
he will restore "good ole American values"

to which values does he refer
in these times of smoke-screen meaning?

thrift
hard work
shared benefits and tolerance...
is this what's implied?

or is it a shoring up of
America's number one value:
to consume?

to become better spenders
here in the land without limits

so full of desire
as the imagery of enticement
works its black magic on our souls

I want this, and I want that!
little boy blue to
blue teenager to
blue-balled adult

taught to want
to have
to hold

to strive for futile perfection:
the perfect body
the perfect face
the perfect house
the perfect spouse
the perfect kids
the perfect job
the perfect car
and then next year's model
on and on...
perpetual consumers
just swipe and sign

yet we're still not happy

and the man with the smiling face
says he wants to be our leader
so he tells us his myth about values

but he says nothing about
tipping points
limits
or sustainability

and he says nothing about
inequality
injustice
exploitation
greed
or the hypocracy inhert
in his party's platform.

happy birthday

they gave me a little party
with big joys
and love drawn from
the all-encompassing roots

more satisfying
than a fete with hundreds

more true
than any purchased statement
between the covers of cardstock

the song rang out to the heavens
with a three-part harmony
perfect off-key adoration
that melted all the china in the cabinet

the shimmering little fires
blown out together
scattering familial hopes
and dreams

the simple gifts
of pure love
that no packed purse can purchase

and best of all
those eyes and smiles
that penetrate

to the depths of my soul
my wife, my son, my daughter
my everything
together on my birthday.

old ways for new days

here is a city
where people are walking
and hardly a car in sight

here is a city
built close together
the grid
and sidewalks just right

here is a city
with trolley cars full
and the workers
they share upbeat words

and here is a city
with tradition and memory
and the voice of the people is heard

with variety
and accents
and flavors to savor
a glass of cold beer
to share with your neighbor

outside this city
are small farms and woods
and the shops are abuzz
with the crafting of goods

the landscape is clear
of billboards and sprawl
and big-box consumption
has no place at all

a railroad line
connects to the world
connects to small farmers
with produce unfurled

and here is a city
where class lines are blurred
and race
in this place doesn't matter

where all coexist
in spaces they share
but no room for fat cats to get fatter

the libraries are full
with people and books
making sense of the faults of their ways

and the parks are filled
with the sounds of laughter
from children who play there all day

and the poets are there
reading words from their works
singing love songs of praise
for their city

shops bubble life
the cafés are all full
and nothing in sight is too gritty

and here is a city
that's so hard to find
in these days of loathing and fear

where rich people hide
behind walls
and guards
and gates to keep nobody near

and here is a city of hope
for the future
old patterns of life hard to see

a planner's dream
just out of reach
out of touch
in the land of TV.

America is

America—
the land of mixed meanings

it is an ideal
an aspiration

it is a starting over
a new beginning

it is a tug-of-war
with neither side winning

it is a role model
for freedom
justice
and waste

America is a hypocrite
a bully on the take
a leader fighting bad guys
many of which we make

America has an English head
and a body almost a mirror
and the body speaks in Spanish
to the head that does not hear

America is where the buffalo roamed
and natives in canoes
and manifest destiny wiped them out
as we came rumbling through

America is polluted air
and factories now all closed
a chemical chicken in every pot
and SUVs on the roads

America hooks up
talks and spends
in ways all emulate
eternally young
eternally dumb
and ever on the take

an altar to the lottery ticket
and sex and drugs and guns
a world of kicks
a world of fear
forever on the run

America is the beginning
and America might be the end

a purveyor of lies
and war
and hope
mixed messages
that we send

America is my blood
my home
my world
and my heartbreak

America is all of us
the world in which we make

America is.

good news

she came into my room last night
soft hand on my shoulder
said something like:
honey...the war is over...the recession has ended...
there's peace and prosperity now...

I said, not now baby...I'm dreaming

but there's more...

I said, come on please
a man can only take so much news
before his soul is irreversibly crushed!

she said, no...this is good news!

I said, look, there is no good news
I check every day, so I know...
there is no good news

she said, you are so dark!
can't you look on the bright side for once?
look...the sun has risen
the sky is blue
and the birds sing out in the trees

I rolled over
and put the pillow over my head
but she kept talking
so I sat up and said:
that sun of which you speak
they say it gives you cancer
through the ozone hole
in the sky
and the blue sky I can't see
through the dirty green smog
blocks my view of the birds with bird flu

so please let me sleep
and get back to my dream
where the world that I see is much better

she said, you don't understand...
it's true!
there's good news today

I said, oh...I understand all right...
I understand...
then I fell back to sleep
dreaming of good news.

meaning

there are more questions
than answers
when you seek eternal certainty

like the philosophers
who consult
angels on pins
about being
and mind
and matter

for proof of Providence
yet no proof but faith
which is nothing
if not another question

and you might ask
why do men start wars
and murder
and forever hate?

and you might think
love is the answer
but the question burns on
while we wait

and you might seek solace
in science and math
where numbers
and proofs seem more solid

but the big bang
is still a theory to bend
toward more questions
and no real answers

and even the simplest of society's ills
beg questions that keep reoccurring

is it poverty
or traffic
where you seek relief?

or justice
or sick nature's churning?

maybe the questions
are closer to home
like how
to keep a loved one
from dying?

but still unanswered
we keep asking why
as our consciousness
seeks out its destiny

but we're ultimately left
to fill in the gaps
with new outlines
or feelings for certainty

and maybe
we couldn't
handle the truth
if the answers
are not what we're after

if there really was
no meaning at all
no bliss in heavenly laughter

or the meaning is waiting out
time to emerge
in the book of life's lost final chapter.

what time is it?

when he looked forward
he couldn't see that far
not as far as when he looked behind

when he thought his thoughts
there were days when it seemed
like an old wise man was in there
shimmering sage musings

and there were days when
that young buck he used to be
was in there laughing
and dreaming
and thinking wild thoughts
from yesteryear's youth

there were days when
he could run for miles
and work out for hours
and perform for thousands
and give big inspired speeches
feeling like a titan

but sometimes
everything ached and creaked
his bleary eyes tired
and his soul feeling
world worn and weary

from the inside
he felt the same
but a pass at the wrong angle
the wrong light
would reveal deep lines
wrinkled eyes he didn't recognize

which made him think about the road ahead
and the roads he'd already traveled

the kids he'd raised
and the careers
and accomplishments

it brought him satisfaction
the knowledge of a life
that left the world a little better
or at least not worse off
never having to step on
or exploit
to succeed

yet he would wonder what's next

was it a smooth stretch to the finish
or an abrupt ending?

or maybe some new plot pivot
to an unexpected chapter?

either way
he was feeling fine
fortified by all that has been
and ready for all that will be

but he knew he wasn't ready
to lie down and say, okay
I'm good

not yet

he needed more time to work on
the mirage of immortality

so he took out a sharp pencil
opened the leather notebook
looked up for a moment
and started writing.